BREAKAWAY

BREAKAWAY

Deliver Value to Your Customers—Fast!

CHARLES L. FRED

JOSSEY-BASS
A Wiley Company
www.josseybass.com

Published by

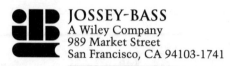

JOSSEY-BASS
A Wiley Company
989 Market Street
San Francisco, CA 94103-1741

www.josseybass.com

Copyright © 2002 by John Wiley & Sons, Inc.

Jossey-Bass is a registered trademark of John Wiley & Sons, Inc.

Jossey-Bass books and products are available through most bookstores. To contact Jossey-Bass directly, call (888) 378-2537, fax to (800) 605-2665, or visit our website at www.josseybass.com.

Substantial discounts on bulk quantities of Jossey-Bass books are available to corporations, professional associations, and other organizations. For details and discount information, contact the special sales department at Jossey-Bass.

We at Jossey-Bass strive to use the most environmentally sensitive paper stocks available to us. Our publications are printed on acid-free recycled stock whenever possible, and our paper always meets or exceeds minimum GPO and EPA requirements.

Library of Congress Cataloging-in-Publication Data

Fred, Charles L., 1961–
    Breakaway : deliver value to your customers—fast!/ Charles L. Fred.
        p.   cm. — (The Jossey-Bass business & management series)
Includes bibliographical references and index.
    ISBN 0-7879-6164-7 (alk. paper)
    1. Customer services–Management.   2. Sales personnel–Training of.   I. Title.   II. Series.
HF5415.5 .F724 2002
    658.8'12—dc21   2002000941

FIRST EDITION

HB Printing   10 9 8 7 6 5 4 3 2 1

The Jossey-Bass
Business & Management Series

To Julie,
my eternal friend, mentor, and partner,
whose support and love made this possible

CONTENTS

ACKNOWLEDGMENTS

The journey to create this book began on January 7, 1993. Julie, my wife and master motivator, left the book *Publish and Flourish* by Garry Schaeffer and Tony Alessandra on my desk, with an encouraging note written on the inside flap. From that moment forward, this book has been under construction. The fact that the book now exists, after nine years of development and research, is truly a result of the people who supported and pushed me forward.

My three wonderful children have encouraged me with smiles through office doors, have scribbled many notes of encouragement, and have graciously given up precious time that could otherwise have been spent together. I owe them so much for their understanding.

Robert Davis, the chief architect of the final version of this book, has been brilliant in his ability to craft a plan I could work with. His coaching and encouragement facilitated the completion of this work. Without his guidance, it would still be a tangled manuscript.

James Keener, my friend and coach, has been with me on this project from the beginning. His early leadership and expertise enabled the research and disparate ideas to take the shape of a manuscript.

I am grateful for Barbara Ellington and her tireless efforts poring over the original manuscript. Her editorial guidance and creative ideas established an innovative direction for the book and the overall message.

The initial research and the notion of a proficiency threshold can be credited to Dr. Stephen Kirkpatrick. His background and genius regarding learning segmentation and the link between learning and performance helped shape many of the ideas in this text.

I would like to acknowledge Dan Guenther and his passion to help me advance as a writer. His past literary success and his encouragement filled my mental fuel tank more than once.

The associates of International Learning Systems and specifically Peggy Steele taught me about the corporate education business. The introductions to many of the references in this book are a result of my experiences with this team, and I thank them for sharing their time and their knowledge.

My time with the people of Omega Performance has reshaped not only this book but my understanding of educational excellence as well. I thank the members of this world-class team for taking me under their wing, teaching me about the financial services industry, and preparing me for the next leg of my journey. Specifically, I thank David Bennett for believing that I could lead the company he cofounded twenty-five years ago and for his untiring support of this book.

I also want to thank the talented team at Jossey-Bass that crafted the final package. Kathe Sweeney, John Bergez, and Jeff Wyneken poured many hours into the finishing touches. They have been a terrific team to work with.

C.L.F.

THE AUTHOR

Charles L. Fred is considered one of the true thought leaders in adult education and learning speed. An internationally known expert on the subjects of leadership, quality, and learning, he has given numerous keynote speeches to the education and telecommunications industries and is helping to transform the adult education industry.

As president and CEO of Avaltus, a global leader in content management software and services for the e-learning industry, he is able to put his ideas to work leading major transformation efforts for both the manufacturing and service industries. His previous roles as the president and CEO of Omega Performance Corporation and as president of Kaplan@Work, a division of Kaplan Education Centers, reinforce his contributions to the adult education industry.

His career began in commercial airplane manufacturing, where during employment with Boeing he held a number of key operational assignments including production engineering supervisor, division systems manager, and general supervisor of the engine-ducting assembly factory. This last experience involved the planning and overseeing of a new multimillion-dollar factory, the transfer of employees from existing facilities, and the daily operation of the new factory, which became one of the premier operations in Boeing's Fabrication Division. Following this work he accepted a challenge by US West to apply aerospace operations technology to the telecommunications industry. As the executive director of network operations, he managed a

XIV | THE AUTHOR

major initiative to improve service and meet access-line growth needs for Colorado, Utah, and Arizona.

He holds a bachelor of science degree in mechanical engineering and technology from Montana State University. He has also completed the Aerospace Manufacturing Program at the University of Washington's Graduate School of Business. He was a nationally ranked NCAA track athlete and continues to compete in corporate races across the country. He lives in Colorado with his wife, Julie, and their three children.

BREAKAWAY

Things may come to those who wait, but only the things left by those who hustle.

ABRAHAM LINCOLN

The Breakaway

T he mile run is a grueling track-and-field race. I had the good fortune to compete in this event during my college days. Since then I've used it as a metaphor to articulate the advantage created by delivering value to customers significantly faster than your competition.

Halfway through the notorious four-lap race, at the beginning of the third lap, a phenomenon called the *breakaway* occurs. Up to this point nearly all runners are still tightly packed together, jockeying for position, cruising at a pace that pushes each runner's pulse between 160 and 190 beats per minute. Lactic acid is accumulating in the large leg muscles, lungs burn as they are filled to capacity and emptied every second, and each runner's brain constantly takes stock of the body's condition even as it craves oxygen itself. At this point, every runner in the pack must make a very tough decision: to summon a burst of speed and attempt to win by breaking away from the other runners or to let others go ahead and rationalize that winning is not really so important.

The breakaway is more than a physical action; it is the most significant mental challenge a runner faces. All the bodily pain and mental anguish must be put aside if one is to break away and win. The breakaway lasts only twenty to thirty seconds, but it is devastating for those who choose to avoid it and inspiring for those who choose to go faster and become part of the lead pack. The leaders move continuously ahead of those left behind, drawing strength from the exhilarating sensation of actually being in a position to win. Their attention is focused outward, toward the future, on reaching the finish line first. Those who follow quickly become consumed with physical exhaustion and the deep disappointment of watching all opportunity for victory vanish. Their attention is focused inward, toward the past, on wondering why they didn't have the strength to stay with the leaders.

A similar phenomenon occurs in the marketplace. Many companies compete in a relatively equal position of market share and growth, with comparable equipment, technological sophistication, and office layouts. Suddenly, one company makes a significant move in as little as two quarters, and few competitors can keep up. Just like the runner who initiates the breakaway, a company that quickly sets itself apart from its competitors becomes outwardly focused on winning. People in these organizations are typically more customer-oriented, have higher morale, and understand how their daily contribution fits into the overall competitive plan. Conversely, organizations that have fallen behind tend to focus on all the internal issues that put them in a losing position. They typically engage in cost reduction measures and reorganization aimed at eliminating employees perceived to be responsible for the deteriorating performance. These are the companies that will continually seek the quick fix.

What enables one company to break away from the rest? I contend that it is increasingly *the ability of people to deliver more value to customers in a shorter period of time*. As the core of our economy continues its shift from the production of goods to the delivery of services, the experience, creativity, and adaptability of the performing human is rapidly becoming the most valuable business asset. Services don't exist until they are performed, and customers judge the service by the performance. Production, delivery, and consumption are often concurrent actions. Therefore, attracting, acquiring, and retaining customers depend on the expertise of the people performing the service. If the time it takes you to deliver a product or service is longer than your competitors', or if your workers are less than proficient, you will lose the race. You will watch from the back of the pack as your competition pulls farther and farther ahead.

A breakaway is initiated by building the basic capacity of an organization and its people to get their jobs done much more quickly and effectively—to deliver greater value to customers faster than the competition. Organizations in the lead set the pace because they have created the wherewithal to develop and sustain a premier workforce. The followers can only focus on the daunting challenge of staying in the race and attempting to keep their workers from defecting to the leader's camp. Rapidly building a proficient workforce may be the single most important movement in an organization's attempt to gain advantage.

What This Book Is About

This book is about how you can create a breakaway in your organization. It represents a new operational focus for business: to transform the way we prepare ourselves to deliver value to customers so that we can deliver it faster and more effectively. The ideas in this book offer a change agenda for anyone who is attempting to create a highly competitive organization in a business world constantly bombarded with increased customer expectations and nimble competition. *Breakaway* is a summary of the core ideas that make one company more competitive than another in creating a proficient workforce. These principles come at a pivotal time in the evolution of today's corporation, as the economy continues to remake itself, new technology revolutionizes processes, and customers rapidly migrate to providers who offer higher value while using less of their time. This book gives the reader a chance to take advantage of this critical time and quickly gain competitive advantage.

Woven into these pages are the results of nearly three hundred interviews with CEOs, technical leaders, training managers, and entry-level employees.[1] The people interviewed represent a diverse mix of companies, from telecommunications firms in western Europe, financial institutions in Southeast Asia and Japan, retail behemoths in the United States and Canada, and manufacturers throughout the world. The interviews were conducted in the spirit of openness regarding the organizations' current processes to develop people, results of recent investments in training and development, and actual financial performance. In turn, I agreed not to reveal specific operational details out of respect for corporate confidentiality and competitive concerns. Their candor gave me new insights into the challenges of leading in an environment where the average life cycle of a digital product is less than six months, where the average worker changes jobs every eighteen months, and where the classroom is often the worst place for developing proficient workers.

A pattern of lessons, key beliefs, and processes emerged from these discussions. Initially, I was seeking a formula, "ten steps" that would enable all organizations to deliver value to customers quickly. My discovery, however, was not a formula or a quick fix. Instead, I found something significantly more important: a reinforcing system that will ultimately establish a new direction for decision makers to follow.

Why This Book Is Needed

More and more, leaders of companies are discovering that the limiting factor in their ability to grow is the scarcity of workers with the most current know-how. Why is this happening even as corporations worldwide continue to downsize their workforce? The answer comes from an economy catalyzed by information and technology and from a new, central role of a worker's know-how in the race to deliver a better-quality product or service in the shortest amount of time. In the days when industry required huge amounts of brawn and little thinking, lack of education and skill wasn't a capacity-constraining problem. Today, however, nearly all jobs require literacy, computer skills, and problem solving. Without them, a person is nearly unemployable. Therefore, leaders today find themselves at the crossroads between having too many people with all of the wrong skills and a training and development process that is far too slow to retrain incumbent workers.

Breakaway was written specifically to deal with this dilemma. The enemy of this situation is time—not the time required for a training event but the total time it takes to prepare a worker to deliver on the promises made to customers. Given the current growth performance of many companies, this time becomes increasingly precious. The challenge is to dramatically reduce this time, retain those great workers by having them deliver new products and services, and regain the growth potential of the enterprise.

The great news is that the majority of people in your organization have an unlimited capacity to learn and perform at the speed of today's economy. When the decision is made to enter the race of daily change, do so with a belief that your people can rapidly become prepared to compete and win. Enter with a passion for taking the people of your organization to the future by helping them gain the knowledge and skills fast enough to realize the awesome competitive power of a breakaway.

Whom This Book Is For

This book is designed for the business reader, to be read in the time it takes to fly from Chicago to San Francisco or Denver to Miami. Its purpose is to excite a wide spectrum of readers. For top managers who may be experiencing the acute pressure of dealing with a distressed organization, this text will give you specific direction to move your organization forward. Those of you who face the challenge of developing and preparing the workforce will discover a revolution in the way workers can learn and the incredible speed with which they become proficient. The majority of chief learning officers, training managers, and instructors that I met while researching the book not only resonate with the ideas in the book, but they have also been refining them. Interestingly enough, one stakeholder group that I have befriended during the course of developing this book is the finance department: cycle time to proficiency and the renewal of the learning curve, both presented in *Breakaway,* enable the financial analyst to grasp the elusive return on investment of the training process. This book is also relevant for students about to begin their careers, the self-employed who are attempting to increase the value of their services, and employees taking charge of their career growth.

How to Use This Book

The heart of this book consists of three new rules presented in a way that redirects the attention of an organization toward delivering value to customers—fast. These rules provide a benchmark, the *proficiency threshold*; a process, *accelerating the accumulation of experience*; and a speedometer, the *cycle time to proficiency*. After clearly establishing the need for a new direction in Chapter One, the next four chapters introduce and define the new rules. These rules fit within a reinforcing system introduced and explained in Chapter Two. Chapters Three, Four, and Five fully develop each rule. Chapter Six examines six styles of breakaway organizations, and Chapter Seven introduces a specific leadership agenda for readers interested in a new, fast-paced direction.

The Intersection of Speed and Expertise

My friend and colleague Paul sat saddle-style with his forearms resting lazily over the back of his chair as he watched the video of our new executive summarizing the current condition of our manufacturing firm. Slowly Paul lowered his head and rested it on his arms. I watched as he and other managers digested and pondered the message.

"The marketplace is changing and driving us to be more competitive," our executive began. "New competitors are targeting our customers and could gain significant market share in a very short period of time. We are too burdened with labor, are too slow in our process improvements, and need contemporary skills to compete effectively. Our customers demand this from us, and they are the reason we must change and change fast.

"Our new strategy calls for streamlining our processes. The game has changed, and we, the leaders of this company, choose to play and protect our market share. We must start to move faster, increase productivity, and delight the customers with outstanding service. If you want to be a part of this new team, get on board with this way of thinking and make the necessary changes immediately."

Paul looked at me with an ashen face, clearly stunned by the message. Just the week before, we had celebrated his twenty-fifth year of service at the company. Times were good, and one could count on being rewarded for hard work and commitment. Now the rules and the game had changed—seemingly overnight.

But these changes had not really occurred that quickly. We had been so busy running the business, so satisfied with the status quo, that the pace of change surrounding our business went unnoticed. We were caught off guard and completely unprepared for what had now become an operational emergency.

Only a month later, after a painful restructuring effort, Paul and I assessed the wreckage of the organization. He and many others had made the decision to take a buyout and retire early. I listened to him articulate his reasons for leaving a place where he had spent half his life. Here was a man who had survived two tours in Vietnam, a painful divorce, and a near-fatal car crash, but he couldn't make it any longer in his job. He rationalized his decision with complaints about his lack of skill in a new economy and an overall lack of energy to deal with constant change.

I watched Paul walk out of the factory that day, his coat slung over one arm, metal lunch box and thermos in the other, pushing past the heavy metal doors as he had for many years, knowing that this time he was not coming back. Instead of a celebratory retirement party and a well-wishing send-off, he joined others at the local bar to ponder an uncertain future.

Many others followed in his footsteps and surrendered, leaving our organization with enormous skill gaps. Each person who left took a chunk of the process and service knowledge of our company. Collectively, we lost the neural system that allowed us to manage the daily variables in our complex business.

Soon thereafter, the company's senior leaders were summoned to attend a strategic meeting to address the critical skill deficiency at the core of the company. We spent the first hour debating the reasons for our crisis. The excuses ranged from a general lack of strategic information about the competition to the notion that we had somehow hired the wrong people ten years ago.

All we knew was that we needed proficient people in a hurry, and we were willing to consider almost any approach to get them. Our training professionals made an impassioned presentation on the need for additional trainers and facilities and proposed an aggressive schedule to get our people up to speed. This heroic proposal required an expensive venture that would leave many of our people still unskilled for the next six months. We simply had too many people without the right skills and not enough time; clearly, it was too late for a conventional plan. Someone then proposed we hire new people with the skills we needed instead of training our remaining workforce. This somehow seemed acceptable under the circumstances: we were all under a lot of pressure to come away from this meeting with a solution.

None of us considered the consequences of this decision until after it was made. We, the leaders of a successful organization, rendered our own people disposable, perceiving them as valuable only if they were lucky enough to have just the right skills at the right time. The pressure to improve our processes quickly was so great that we ignored the most crucial process of all— enabling the people in our organization to gain the skills to make the new processes work. And somehow we had come to the conclusion that our people were not capable of learning fast enough to catch up.

The ultimate cost of this false assumption was absolute chaos in the workplace and a dramatic decrease in our company's stock value due to exorbitant staffing costs and customer base erosion. We seemed surprised when new workers soon exhibited skill gaps similar to those of the old workers they had replaced, as processes changed and new equipment quickly surpassed the new workers' knowledge. The ugly cycle of dumping those with obsolete skills continued until we finally realized that the key to survival and growth was in retaining and developing our own people, relying on their ability to learn fast in order to deliver value to the customer.

This story illustrates the fundamental truth underlying this book: our economy is now driven by the connection of speed and expertise. Today start-ups thirst for the critical skills to build a business, knowing that if they lack proficient workers to enter the marketplace and immediately gain customer attention, they are dead. Blue chips attempt the daunting task of preparing a workforce to support the new digital world while keeping the old processes alive for millions of customers who still need them. Nearly everything we thought we knew about the economy ten years ago is now open to question. But one thing is clear: the basic ability of an enterprise to survive and grow is a function of know-how—of how quickly it can get its people to learn something new and transfer this knowledge into value for

> Speed is now equal to quality in its value to consumers and—for the delivery of a service—consistently outweighs price.
>
> Humans, with the knowledge and skills that enable them to deliver on the promises made to customers, are the primary source of economic value in business today.

its customers. In our rapidly changing marketplace, it is deadly to be comfortable with yesterday's pace for learning. Humans, with the knowledge and skills that enable them to deliver on the promises made to customers, are without doubt the primary source of economic value in business today. A proficient worker—armed with the tools to learn as fast as the economy changes—becomes the catalytic ingredient for a business to grow.

The Need for Speed

Fred Smith, the founder of Federal Express, changed more than the way a package is delivered. He, and others who followed, fundamentally changed the expectations of consumers. No longer are quality and price the only drivers of competition. Speed has now become a primary variable in consumers' perception of value. Consumers expect and demand smart employees to handle their requests immediately—with one call to the toll-free service line, instant availability of inventory, and immediate and accurate information. Speed of service, product availability, and information are becoming critical factors in a company's ability to compete.

> The most important—and most vulnerable—connection between strategy and execution is the actual performance of people.

Pick any service offered today and consider how your expectations of availability and delivery have changed. These expectations are continuously reinforced as consumers reward providers that offer services faster than the competition. Speed is now equal to quality in its value to consumers and—for the delivery of a service—consistently outweighs price. The source of the demand for speed is consumers, and their definition of value consistently includes time—their time.

This change in our perception of time has been accelerated by information readily available at the click of a mouse or the touch of a button. For example, until recently, the average time to apply for and receive approval for a standard home mortgage was five working days. Nearly every banking institution operated at this pace, and banks did not agonize about offering faster loan approval as a part of their value proposition. Instead, their focus was on accurate service, product differentiation, and rate offerings. Today, however, loan approvals are nearly instantaneous, and the consumer's expectations regarding the speed of all of the follow-on services necessary to complete a loan transaction continue to escalate. Technology has fundamentally altered consumers' perception of what constitutes value in financial services.

The need to deliver value to customers faster has moved well past the consumer model and now permeates every enterprise whose customers value their time. Business-to-business product and service companies are now under great pressure to deliver value rapidly. Wholesale utility providers, Internet infrastructure manufacturers, and even the big consulting firms are grappling with the consequences of their lack of speed. Their destiny, like that of the fast-moving consumer service businesses, is now inextricably tied to how quickly they can retool to meet the speed demands of the enterprise customer.

Well over a decade ago, firms began to grasp the advantage of bringing products to market faster than the competition.

Companies that have adopted speed to market as an operating principle have found that it catalyzes growth in their profits and loyalty in their workers. Today, leaders are beginning to understand that advantage lies not just in the faster development of new products and services but also in the faster development in the expertise of the people who deliver those products and services. Great improvements have been made in the science and process of developing new products, but the real opportunity to outperform the competition comes from the up-to-date know-how of the worker who serves the customer. The best enhancement and extension of a brand in a knowledge-based economy is not the look and feel of marketing collateral and products, but rather the reputation and knowledge of the people selling and servicing those products. Proficient employees leave a long and lasting impression on customers. This impression, coupled with a strong brand, can build loyalty and retention levels that are impossible for the competition to match. Expertise may therefore become the most recognizable element of a company's brand.

> Speed to proficiency is more than a theoretical advantage: it is the most devastating competitive weapon in a world where the competitive forces of scale, automation, and capital are subordinate to the power of a proficient workforce.

The advantages of placing a product or service in the hands of a customer before the competition does are so glaringly clear that one would assume that ensuring worker proficiency in the delivery process would be a high business priority. More often than not, however, the proficiency of the workers who deliver or support the new offering does not satisfy the customer. Marketing human know-how is only a competitive advantage if a system is in place to actually create proficient workers. Marketers can fool the wise consumer only once. A company with a reputation for uninformed or disenfranchised workers will have a very tough time reversing the negative perception already created.

Speed to Proficiency

It is obvious that a new system for rapidly developing the workforce is needed, and yet many business leaders are preoccupied with activities that seem much more urgent. They overlook the fact that the most important—and most vulnerable—connection between strategy and execution is the actual performance of people. Senior managers have consistently failed to consider the capacity of their people to learn faster.[1] The intersection between work and learning, between an individual's job and the promise of swift service to the consumer, poses a significant challenge to the leaders of today's organizations. In this economy, the importance of a skilled, proficient force of workers, capable of decision making, problem solving, and self-direction in handling the primary tasks of their jobs, will continually escalate. Most of the traditional methods to develop these capabilities in an organization move too slowly. Staying competitive demands that people learn faster than is possible with traditional learning models. Keeping the speed requirement from crashing into the training department will require leaders to refocus on the basic performance capacity of the organization and to seek creative ways to help workers match their learning process with the speed of change.

The economy of speed offers a new and incremental advantage. Any organization that can quickly develop a critical mass of proficient workers will always be in the lead pack and in a position to dominate the marketplace. Proficient workers speed things up: organizational change, operational improvement, problem solving, and delivery of service all happen faster. When you shorten the time it takes for workers to become proficient, the capital and resources required to introduce a new product, maintain operations and infrastructure, and perform a service are also proportionally reduced. I call this *speed to proficiency,* and the concept is central to this book. Speed to proficiency is more than a theoretical advantage: it is the most devastating competitive weapon in a world where the competitive forces of scale, automation, and capital are subordinate to the power of a proficient work force.

Put your skepticism on hold and ask yourself if you and the people in your company can reach proficiency at the speed they need to compete and prevail against the competition. Can your current system for developing people fulfill the growth requirements of your shareholders, satisfy anxious customers, and excite your workers enough to keep them? If not, I offer new ideas to help improve the pace of performance, the speed with which you can change, and the overall competitiveness of your firm.

CHAPTER TWO

Three New Rules for a New World

> The overwhelming majority of corporate training
>
> and development initiatives produce results
>
> no different from my problem-solving class.

One day when I was a senior manager at the telecommunications firm US West, I was sifting through my office mail when I noticed a handwritten note among the stack of laser-printed documents. The note, sent by a frontline network technician named Kyle, was written on the back of a blank work order.

Dear Mr. Fred,

I recently attended the training class you've sponsored on Team Problem Solving. I know your intentions are good, but I wanted to give you some feedback.

I work ten hours a day out of my truck. Nearly everything I need to complete a work order fits someplace in this rig. The instructor said to keep the class materials handy over the next few weeks for reference. Where do I put this three-ring binder? To be honest with you, I highly doubt that I will ever refer to these materials. Would you like them back for the next class to use?

I think your vision of us needing problem-solving and productivity skills is OK, but did you really think this class would make us better at bringing service to our customers?

Our biggest problem or skill shortage is knowing how to install these new remote terminals. It takes twice as long [to install them] as the old ones. We keep telling customers that we will get them telephone service faster, but the only training we get is this problem-solving crap. Every day I have to face the homeowner that is waiting for phone service. If you want to help, get us the training we need to get these people hooked up faster!

Thanks for listening. I just thought you should know that we don't think much of this kind of training.

Kyle

When Kyle sent me this note, the Public Utilities Commission was investigating US West's poor performance on "held orders" —accounts for which we could not deliver basic telephone service to customers in thirty days or less. Network technicians like Kyle were under intense pressure to correct this embarrassing problem and were routinely working overtime. Compounding this situation was a fourteen-state promotion of US West's new service quality initiative that promised customers dramatic improvements in service.

Seven months before receiving Kyle's letter, I had decided to embark on a divisionwide training program to help frontline workers solve problems more quickly and effectively, in part because our annual employee survey had indicated a general lack of problem-solving skills among the workforce. It seemed obvious that our employees needed problem-solving training. Kyle's note, however, made what seemed obvious look outright ridiculous. Training in problem-solving skills might possibly have helped some employee solve some problem sometime in the future, but workers *right now* lacked the specific skills to deliver what the company was promising to the customer today. Moreover, after looking into how much training our network technicians received for technical service skills, I discovered that little or none was being provided—indeed, almost all of our training budget was set aside for management development, rather than training the front line. Considering how little training the technicians were receiving, the fact that most of it wasn't linked directly to providing value to the customer was appalling.

Prior to Kyle's missive, I considered the problem-solving course to be an enlightened management action that was directly aligned with our company's belief in lifelong learning, a universal subsidy to the organization. Following the conventional wisdom of the training industry and modern corporate culture, I believed I was investing in workers and in the future of the company. But Kyle made it clear that the investment was wasted—and indeed, had crowded out the critical training that *was* needed. I also realized that even *had* the training been linked to delivering value to the customer, it still probably would have failed because it would have relied on traditional training techniques that have little to do with how people actually learn to do real things on the job. Classroom learning and three-ring binders may be the preferred tools of the training industry, but as Kyle pointed out, they are no better than a nuisance in real life. On top of all this, I realized that my course was far too slow to deal with the urgency of Kyle's—and my—problem. Getting frontline technicians up to speed fast was imperative, yet traditional training courses required a six-month ramp-up period, and after the training was over, there was no way of knowing whether we had reached our destination.

In an instant I could see a different path. The promise made to customers—in this case, the promise of fast, high-quality telephone service—should be the driving force behind investment in training and development. Kyle should have received carefully designed on-the-job technical training for installing the new equipment, with elements of problem solving built in, in order to get service to customers faster. The training would have relied not on classroom theory and three-ring binders but on the accumulation of real-world experience in installing the new units in a variety of challenging circumstances. The measure of the success of the training would have been how much faster Kyle and other network technicians could deliver phone service to customers. The payoff would have been unmistakable—a direct advantage for customers, employees, and the company.

This experience illustrates the three fundamental themes of this book: the principles of the breakaway.

First, training and development must be linked directly to the delivery of value to customers. If businesses fully grasped this concept, it would produce a fundamental shift—a Copernican revolution—in how they trained and developed their people.

Second, training and development must adopt new learning techniques that focus workers on quickly accumulating real-world experience delivering on the promise to customers. That most of the vast modern training and development industry fails, day in and day out, to do this is a true scandal—and an enormous opportunity for businesses that can succeed at it.

Third, the effectiveness of training and development must be measured by the speed with which workers can deliver the promised value to customers. Employees need to be brought to proficiency fast because customers won't wait. When a company can accelerate the delivery of value to its customers by accelerating the speed with which workers learn to deliver that value, it will realize the competitive advantage of the breakaway.

Let us now examine these themes in the context of what is wrong with most current training and development and then explore three new rules that can transform businesses and create the breakaway.

Linking Development to Delivery of Value

The breakaway begins with the understanding that businesses exist to deliver value to their customers, and if they do it well, then shareholders, employees, and customers will all be rewarded. The concept of a "value proposition," the ultimate promise made to customers, has become common marketing language in most organizations. Great strides have been made by businesses over the past decade in understanding and defining the "value chain," the collective process by which each enterprise creates value for its customers. Many organizations are now capable of defining and measuring this process not only for obvious functions such as product development and marketing but also for functions further removed from the customer such as finance and accounting. Businesses are increasingly able to know which of their activities are most profitable and deliver the greatest value to customers and make investments based on this knowledge.

Remarkably, most businesses have not applied anything close to this level of scrutiny to their investments in training and development. The ideals of the training and development industry— investing in the future, the power of knowledge, lifelong learning, to name but a few—are so grand and compelling that it somehow seems ungrateful to ask whether training and development are profitable activities when compared to other things in which a business might invest its time and money.

But the truth is that the overwhelming majority of corporate training and development initiatives produce results no different from my problem-solving class at US West. Participants in that training learned the latest ideas in teamwork and problem solving, and most left the class insisting that they found the training at least somewhat useful and could perform the skills they learned in the class. What they could not do, as Kyle so candidly and eloquently informed me, was to apply these new skills to solve the single greatest problem they faced: delivering what was promised to the customer. Since businesses exist to deliver value to customers, it's safe to say that the training was a poor investment. Some might even say it did more harm than good. The fact that the overwhelming majority of modern corporate training and development shared in my failure was small consolation.

Experiences like this happen thousands of times each day in America. Businesses spend billions of dollars each year on classes just like mine. But few ask whether any of this investment delivers value to the customer and how much the business benefits from the investment. Few businesses have recognized the development of their people as a key link in the value chain. More precisely, training is rarely positioned as the primary means to deliver on the promises made to customers. The training of the workforce is usually viewed as a necessary chore or sometimes as an enlightened perk rather than a strategically critical link in the value chain. Although marketing, product development, branding, and promotion are all considered vital priorities for revenue growth, the ability of the workforce to deliver is almost always a secondary consideration. The reactionary design and development of training has become an operational habit—a habit that for most of us seems perfectly normal.

> The training of the workforce is usually viewed as a necessary chore or sometimes as an enlightened perk, rather than a strategically critical link in the value chain.

Accumulating Experience

The second problem with modern training and development stems directly from the first. Midway through the twentieth century, unsystematic on-the-job apprenticeships were replaced with professionally designed training events, which now make up the bulk of U.S. corporate training.[1] By separating training from work, newly minted training professionals hoped to apply new adult learning theories in pursuit of new standards of employee competence. Event-based training was also convenient for learning designers because they could create a one-size-fits-all class and then herd workers together in a single session. In our current frame of thinking, little business training occurs outside the defined boundaries of a learning event.

A critical effect of this transformation has been to disconnect training and development from the delivery of value to the customer. For today's learning professional, the goal of learning events is to help business learners achieve abstract levels of "competence" in skills and concepts that learning professionals believe are prerequisites for performance. The purpose of my problem-solving course, for example, was not to solve the specific problem workers faced in installing new units in order to deliver promised service to customers but rather to introduce workers to general problem-solving ideas and skills in the hope that they might find some of them useful back on the job.

The flaw in this approach is that it is based on a profound misapprehension of how adults really learn. Much of the roughly $60 billion spent each year on training is lost because most of what is presented in the training event is not thoroughly learned and what is learned is not retained.[2] Even though few managers truly believe in instant proficiency, their attitudes toward training often seem to contradict their innate common sense. They target nearly all their training effort and investment on the initial training event. If decision makers knew that nearly 80 percent of their investment is lost within forty-eight hours of each class, they would take this problem more seriously. With little or no practice of the training material, retention falls at an accelerating rate. G. V. Goddard calls this rate the "forgetting curve."[3] Figure 2.1 shows the rapid loss of retention and the risks for retaining so little that proficiency is never attained.

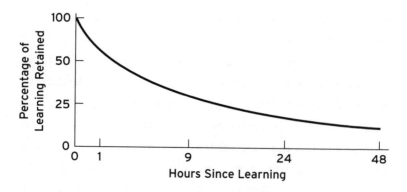

FIGURE 2.1. The Forgetting Curve.

Quite simply, learners forget what they have learned before it can be practiced in real life. In traditional training, this is often addressed by saying that classroom learning needs to be "reinforced" on the job or it will be lost. The implication is that the job should change to support learning. In fact, it is the learning that needs to change to support the job. The problem isn't simply a lack of reinforcement. The problem is that learning is not fundamentally integrated with strategic business needs, and so the employee's educational experiences never reach the critical mass required for the training to be effective. For learning to "stick," for knowledge to be retained, the learner needs a series of learning experiences in close proximity. In other words, knowledge is a waste if it is not converted into performance within a very short time. And unless the performance is immediately and directly connected to the delivery of value to customers, it will never happen, because it will inevitably be pushed aside by urgent things that *are* explicitly linked to the delivery of value to customers.

What's missing from our current learning systems? I'll go into more detail later, but let's go through the highlights now. Adults move through four phases as they learn. In the first phase, new information is *introduced* to our cognitive processes. This may be information about a new product or new service, or it may be a new theory. We progress into the second phase, called *assimilation,* in which the human memory combines the new information with previous experiences and learning. In phase 3, we *translate* the new information and our previous knowledge into a job function or a particular application.

> Learning is not fundamentally integrated with strategic business needs, and so the employee's educational experiences never reach the critical mass required for the training to be effective.

At this point, most of us can understand how the new information relates to our job and what needs to be done to actually perform, but we still can't perform. Therefore, the fourth and most crucial phase is the *accumulation of experience* with the new information. Converting knowledge into performance requires experience. Across the world, the lion's share of training dollars are tied up in the first three phases, leaving the accumulation of experience mostly to chance. Yet this fourth phase will dictate whether an employee can actually deliver on the promises made to a customer.

The accumulation of experience, most often completely ignored by professional instructional designers, is by far the most important step toward ensuring proficiency and delivering value to the customer. Without it, a decision maker can bank on the fact that nearly all of the investment will end up wasted and that significant additional time and money will be needed as employees grapple in the workplace to find the practice and accumulation of experience that were absent in the initial training.

Focusing on Speed

The third problem with traditional training and development is that it is too slow to meet the needs of customers and to achieve the critical mass necessary to accumulate experience. Think about the sequential method of the traditional employee training session. A training need appears, a course is found, and over a period of time employees are trained. Some will take the course many months before they need to apply the skills, while others wait until well after the training is needed. The number of students per session is dictated by the availability of both learners and teacher. But today most businesses cannot operate in this kind of "batch" mode. They need to place proficient workers when and where the need exists. In today's environment, few people have time for extracurricular events of any kind, let alone training. Much has changed from the days when you could "schedule" people into training and provide someone to back them up on the job. Faced with the competition, few managers can afford to take employees away from customers or the front line. Business leaders are aware that it takes too long to train workers in the traditional method, but most are using an old set of rules to fix the problem.

"Training takes too long!" This is the characteristic response of frustrated decision makers to current training solutions, which are simply too slow for the breakneck pace of business today. Yet all too often the solution is shortsighted: simply truncate the time it takes to get people trained. This reactive solution assumes that learning can occur instantaneously, in a onetime event. To accommodate the need for an increased pace, classes that were once designed for five consecutive days of delivery have now been condensed to two days, maybe three. Each time a "quick fix" is applied and a course is shortened, there is an illusion that learning has occurred, and in less time. Statements like "We are training our people faster" corroborate this false assumption. Beyond this compression of class time, there are usually no other innovations in course content or design.

The result is like drinking from a fire hose: the rush of data is overwhelming, not enough information is retained to apply back on the job, and there is no opportunity to accumulate experience. The condensed version of the course wastes not only two days of valuable learning time but also two days of service or production. When people return to the job, expected efficiencies do not materialize because little, if any, learning actually occurred during the compressed course. Strangely, this failure often goes undetected because results are rarely measured back on the job.

The implications of this are staggering. Imagine a service company receiving an order for a particular service through its inbound call center. The order fulfillment process records the order and places it in a delivery queue but then abandons any follow-up on the performance or delivery of the service—no one ever checks to see if the service was actually completed and in a way that was acceptable to the customer. This company's chances of survival are slim. But this is precisely the circumstance in which businesses and organizations delivering traditional training events find themselves.

When the goal of training is to deliver value to customers fast—whether that means to serve the customer directly, improve the quality of products, or support others in the business—then priorities for learning and skill development by definition become merged with strategic business decisions because the training clearly and directly serves the organization's reason for existence. Managers therefore approach the problem as they would any other operational constraint and apply resources directly to the workers who need it most. In contrast, when the primary purpose is to benevolently expose great numbers of people to a course whose outcomes are expressed in grand but vague terms (my problem-solving course again being typical), the operational purpose is invariably lost in the complex process of moving a mass of people through an event.

The great news about the changes in our world and our economy is that they play right into the strengths of humans. Constant advances in technology will automate many repetitive activities required in the manufacturing and service sectors and will facilitate the movement of information, enabling people to innovate, create, and serve, all of which will become the growth and value drivers of our future.

The Three New Rules

If you were to pause and think seriously about the three things that can bring people in your organization to proficiency faster than anything else, what would they be? For nearly a decade, I have asked this question of business leaders around the globe. In answering the question, none of them cited needs analysis research or a specific instructional design model, and only a handful suggested a training course. Instead, they were passionate about getting employees into practice sessions quickly, using new technology to bring information to workers, and breaking new information into sound bites while linking it with daily work activities. Most of these leaders were also excited about creating an environment where they could see the speed of their progress manifest in people who dazzle customers and exceed organizational expectations. Unfortunately, most of these discussions ended with an admission that the current training system in their organization is nothing even close to what they described as "fast."

> When the goal of training is to deliver value to customers fast, then priorities for learning and skill development by definition become merged with strategic business decisions.

The following rules define a new model for human performance that will help advance the learning efforts of these leaders toward fulfilling their passion for speed (see Figure 2.2). The model has been pounded into shape by a number of colleagues who have worked through the nuances of the original theory and put the rules into practice. This model has enabled organizations to bring people to proficiency up to 80 percent faster than the traditional methods. As I discuss in Chapter Six, however, no single recipe or step-by-step process will drive speed to proficiency; speed will also depend on a number of additional issues relating to leadership and enthusiasm. Therefore, this model does not propose a formula, but rather it helps establish a new orientation centered on using speed and expertise to deliver value to

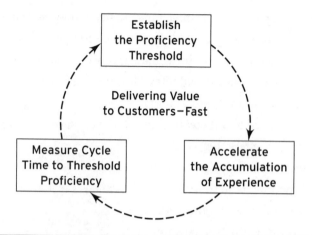

FIGURE 2.2. A New Model for Human Performance.

customers—*fast*. The next three chapters of this book illuminate the following rules:

1. Establish the proficiency threshold.
2. Accelerate the accumulation of experience.
3. Measure the cycle time to threshold proficiency.

Rule 1: Establish the Proficiency Threshold

To be able to deliver value to customers, leaders must clearly understand that growth in the new economy will demand a different way of looking at the human contribution. Today's leader must clearly understand that the worker is no longer a commodity, as technology takes over that role. A leader's real job, then, is to create a team of performers who can deliver value to customers fast, and the workers' real job is to know when they have achieved the proficiency to deliver on what has been promised.

To achieve the rapid delivery of value to customers, an absolutely clear picture of the value proposition must be created, and all performance must be connected to it. What specific promise does the enterprise make to customers? Exactly how do training and development support the delivery of that value? How will we know if training has successfully delivered value? What will we do if it hasn't?

The point at which a person can deliver the promised value is called the *proficiency threshold,* and for the remainder of this book, I will refer to threshold proficiency as a critical point in a company's ability to compete. This milestone must be defined and understood before any precious time is spent on learning activities. Once the overarching value proposition becomes the focus of training, the development of people to deliver on the promise becomes significantly less complex. In today's economy, all professional development activities must advance the delivery of the proposition. Any activities that are not clearly tied to the proposition should be questioned. It becomes a simple litmus test: Will this help us deliver on the promise to customers or not?

> If you were to pause and think seriously about the three things that can bring people in your organization to proficiency faster than anything else, what would they be?

Rule 2: Accelerate the Accumulation of Experience

Accumulating enough experience to deliver on the value proposition takes a performer directly to the heart of what matters most in business learning. Employees can test concepts, alter approaches, fail quickly and recover quickly, and ultimately gain the needed experience to perform. Nothing about this method, however, should be left to chance. When done correctly, this phase is as strictly designed as the classroom. Imagine working and accumulating experience in an environment where your performance coach sits in the adjacent cubicle or is immediately available online. Short, reinforcing modules and reference materials are readily available on your browser, one phone call will net an immediate answer to a question, and a manager checks in to assess your progress. Focusing on the accumulation of experience is a critical shift from traditional training and is absolutely necessary to achieving breakaway performance. This reformation makes possible the true advantage for an enterprise in today's competitive environment—a reduction in the time it takes to deliver on the promises made to the marketplace and to analysts, shareowners, and employees.

Rule 3: Measure the Cycle Time to Threshold Proficiency

Cycle time to threshold proficiency is a metric that will drive new competitive behaviors. The metric helps redefine the development of people in the context of the delivery of value and of time—in this case, the time it takes for individuals to prepare themselves to perform. In essence, if everyone is connected to the value proposition, everyone must also deliver on the promise fast, before someone else does. This metric alone will have a profound effect on an organization's ability to compete. The very act of measuring cycle time to proficiency communicates that learning speed is an integral part of delivering value to customers fast. Improving the organization's cycle time to proficiency is the secret to the breakaway.

The Challenge

Remember the good old days? The Alfred P. Sloan Museum in Flint, Michigan, is a fantastic reminder of the great business days of the past. Its automotive artifacts are a testament to the economic opulence created by the automotive industry. From the 1930s to the 1970s, General Motors was the model for how great businesses were run, and Alfred P. Sloan was arguably the most powerful businessman on earth. During this time, GM defined the game of business and its rules. Its success came from an economy of scale, owning the supply chain, and lifetime employment.

Today, Bill Gates and Michael Dell define the game and the rules. Within a very short time, they too may have a museum like Sloan's. The game of business is changing very rapidly. It took more than forty years for a new order to overtake the business model inherited from GM. Some commentators argue that Microsoft has already lost its dominance as the ideal model. If past economic changes are any indication of the future, businesses who seek to play the new game by the new rules will at the very least be in a position to recover when the contest changes again. The new rules will test some deep-seated beliefs about adult training and learning. I challenge those of you who are responsible for the competitiveness of your organization to reorient your thinking toward a new way of developing people, to build and develop a workforce that can anticipate and adapt as quickly as the economy changes, and to break away from the competition.

CHAPTER THREE

Rule 1: Establish the Proficiency Threshold

> What promise is made to your customers?
>
> What role do your people play in delivering on that promise?
>
> Which of your competitors makes a similar promise?
>
> What happens if your competition delivers on that promise first?

Recently, I was searching for a portable projector to use for giving presentations when I travel—some of the newer units are compact and light enough to carry on a plane. A spacious advertisement in *USA Today* drew my attention: "We provide smart features that can save you even more money down the line. Want full specs? Just give us a ring." At the bottom of the page was a toll-free number.

I called and inquired into some of the product specifications. "I don't have that kind of information," the employee replied. "Would you like to talk with one of our technical reps?" After being transferred and put on hold for several minutes, the technical representative told me, "I'm kind of new here and am not sure what those exact specifications are. Would you like me to send you one of our technical brochures? Have you by chance looked at our Web site? It may have some information that will answer your question." "No," I replied, "I think I will move on." I declined to mention that the only reason I called was to save time by quickly obtaining technical information about the product over the phone, as promised in the advertisement.

A competing organization with proficient workers would put this company out of business. I use the term *proficiency* to describe the ability of an individual worker to produce the promised value for customers. In the case of my telephone call, a proficient worker not only would be able to deliver the promised information but also would leave the indelible impression that this was an organization that delivered on its promises to customers. When customers have so many options in choosing providers, any gap between what has been promised and what is delivered will provoke most customers to switch. Survival for any company today hinges on the connection between the promise made to customers and the ability of the workforce to deliver on that promise. The corollary is that fostering this ability must be at the heart of our training and development efforts.

Delivering on the Promise to Customers

Consider the following four questions to establish a framework for understanding the relationship between the promise you make to customers and the ability, or proficiency, that your workers need in order to deliver on that promise.

- *What promise is made to your customers?* Seek and find the commitments and promises that have been made to your customers. This discovery is often called the "value proposition" and should focus squarely on the customer.
- *What role do your people play in delivering on that promise?* Very few promises are fulfilled without the critical involvement

of people. In a business that offers intangible services, every promise is fulfilled by a person; the personal service *is* the product. A deep understanding of how effective your employees currently are in fulfilling the promise to the customer is the first step in identifying what development and learning efforts will be required for them to truly succeed.

• *Which of your competitors makes a similar promise?* The truth is that when you compare value propositions, marketing collateral, and service offerings, there's often a remarkable similarity among products and services in today's market.

• *What happens if your competition delivers on that promise first?* This is the crucial organizing question for businesses that choose to compete with both speed and proficiency. Simply asking this question will inspire a series of conversations about the ability of your workforce to do battle. This inquiry will also cause significant anxiety as you ponder your vulnerability to a nimble, proficient competitor.

Today's business environment demands a new perspective on employee development—a shift from traditional education as a training event to a new kind of education that on every level augments the delivery of value to customers. In the future, this focus will be a fundamental driver of competitiveness in a firm. The time a worker spends in any form of learning must be tied directly to the promises made to customers. When the connection is tight, learners immediately understand their role in delivering value to the customer, and the objective of learning and performing is literally defined by what the organization is attempting to do for its customer. Again, the ability to deliver the promised value to customers is what I mean by proficiency, and the first rule for creating it is to establish what I call the *proficiency threshold*.

What Is the Proficiency Threshold?

It is critical to distinguish proficiency from the objective of traditional training, the acquisition of knowledge. Proficiency requires doing, application, and results. Knowledge, the end product of most training, is by itself inadequate; knowledge alone will not enable an employee to perform. A person can obtain knowledge, even advanced knowledge, and still be unable to perform satisfactorily to meet a customer's need. Think of fresh college graduates entering the job market with heads full of recently acquired learning: few will be able to immediately step into an assignment and begin to add value. The same is true of any worker who has attended a lecture or read a book. Of course, proficiency requires knowledge, but it also requires that this knowledge come alive and be transformed through experience. Proficiency is a more potent objective than training and knowledge creation: proficiency is the use of knowledge in action for the purpose of producing value for a customer.

The proficiency threshold, therefore, is the exact moment when a worker can convert knowledge through action into the promised value for the customer. The proficiency reached at this moment can be measured, and it can't be faked. Defining the precise moment when a worker can perform well enough to deliver the promised value to customers is the crucial action for an organization to execute on its competitive strategy.

For individual employees, the proficiency threshold is the

moment at which both they and the organization know that value can be delivered to customers. At first glance that may seem obvious, but think how often businesses seem confused about what proficiency their employees need in order to serve customers. For an example, all we have to do is return to Kyle, the technician at US West whom you met in Chapter Two. In that situation, my vision of the problem-solving skills needed by front-line workers had little or nothing to do with the urgent problems they actually faced installing new terminals in order to deliver the value promised to customers. The threshold level of proficiency is crucial to competitive advantage because it is the point at which an employee begins to contribute value in a particular job or task.

The point at which workers *together* can create and deliver value to the customer, the collective proficiency threshold, is the moment when the business's strategy and plans become executed. The proficiency threshold is reached when the sales and marketing team can sell and advertise value to customers with confidence, when orders are filled on time, when services meet customer expectations, and when the management team is leading as envisioned. By definition, the proficiency threshold links an individual worker to the vision and strategy of the organization in the context of his or her performance.

A key point here is that not all jobs in an organization require the same level of proficiency with respect to all the possible tasks each worker may perform; the threshold level of proficiency depends on the position and the task at hand. Rarely would a senior sales manager, for example, need to have the technical financial proficiency of an accounting specialist; the manager probably needs to be proficient only in using sales reporting systems. Conversely, an accounting specialist need only understand the basic principles of the corporate sales strategy, whereas a senior manager needs to know the minute details of that strategy.

The fastest method to get the collective organization to the proficiency threshold, therefore, is to clearly identify the specific components of each job that help deliver on the company's promise to the customer and to define the level of proficiency required for each of these components. The proficiency threshold may in fact be at one of three different levels, depending on the role of the employee: literacy, fluency, or mastery.

> The time a worker spends in any form of learning must be tied directly to the promises made to customers.

Literacy is the ability to articulate knowledge in the context of one's job. This is the level usually attained during well-designed traditional training events. For certain jobs, literacy may be the threshold level of proficiency—the accountant just mentioned, for example, is proficient if he understands the corporate sales strategy at the level of literacy—but for most primary tasks in most jobs, it is insufficient.

Fluency is the ability to perform a task with ease. It can be attained only through actual practice and application. It is a function of the amount of experience accumulated over a period of time. Fluency marks the threshold level of proficiency required for the essential functions of most jobs, and yet the vast majority of traditional training activities do not ensure that learners reach this level.

Mastery is achieved with additional experience, when one acquires true expertise. This level is generally beyond what is necessary to deliver value to customers and therefore represents an unnecessary goal for training and development (although for certain jobs that demand flawless execution without fail, fluency may not be enough and mastery may represent threshold proficiency).

By identifying the proficiency threshold for each critical task of each position in an organization, decision makers take the first step toward formulating a precise strategy to develop the workforce faster. This allows them to determine how best to use scarce time and financial resources to achieve the crucial initial level of performance. In this process, proficiency across an organization is viewed strategically rather than tactically.

Threshold Proficiency in Action

Let's take as an example a division of a company that offers products for the home office market—computer hard drives, printers, modems, memory, and monitors—and is launching a new series of products and services and needs to train its people. Traditionally, corporate trainers would develop a course to educate the sales and marketing group (and often other employees as well), stuffing into this one course anything and everything that anyone might need to learn about the technical specifications, capabilities, features, and benefits of the new line. The course would be designed to bring the average sales and marketing employee to a level of mastery in one lengthy mass session—a vain effort that would barely make the employee literate and would leave the organization with a sales force far below the level of proficiency needed to perform effectively in front of skeptical customers. Figures 3.1 and 3.2 illustrate the typical expectations and typical results of this approach.

In contrast, through strategic identification of the threshold level of proficiency, an organization not only can bring its sales and marketing employees to proficiency more quickly but also can for the first time define the proficiency level that other employees must achieve for the successful introduction of new products and services. Figure 3.3 illustrates how threshold proficiency is targeted for different positions in this company. Note that very few employees will need to achieve mastery as a result of this training; only the sales coaches and mentors (about 5 percent of the total group) need to reach this level as their initial threshold (sales management, customer service, administrative support, and legal staff need to achieve varying lesser levels of proficiency in the features and benefits of the new products and services). Most members of the sales and marketing team need to reach a fluency level, and they can achieve this with a short training course followed by rapid rounds of practice and

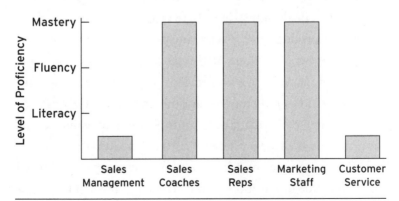

FIGURE 3.1. Expectations of Traditional Sales Training.

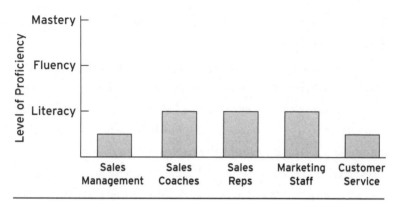

FIGURE 3.2. Results of Traditional Sales Training.

rapid real-work accumulation of experience. Not only are resources applied more strategically, but workers can very quickly reach the literacy level in a myriad of ways made possible by today's advancements in technology, such as Web-based training.

Threshold Proficiency and the Value Chain

In their book *The Balanced Scorecard,* Robert Kaplan and David Norton define a common set of attributes that organize value propositions in all industries. These propositions fall into three categories: product and service, image, and relationships.[1] As shown in Figure 3.4, these attributes help map how the value proposition relates to the worker. This map helps decision makers understand—in many cases for the first time—the relationship between the organization's proposition of value to the customer and the true proficiency needs of the worker.

Take, for example, the home office solution company discussed earlier. Its value propositions to potential consumers fit into these three categories. Failure to deliver in any one of the categories

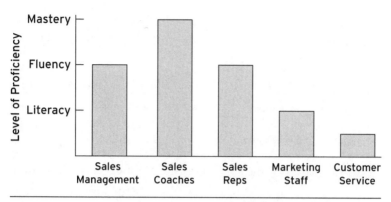

FIGURE 3.3. Strategically Selecting the Proficiency Threshold.

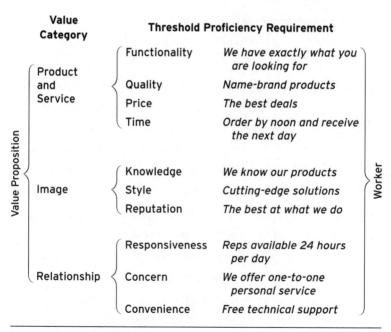

FIGURE 3.4. Linking the Value Proposition to the Worker.

because of a nonproficient workforce will leave this organization vulnerable to the competition and could undermine any chance of building a long-term relationship with a customer.

> The proficiency threshold is the exact moment when a worker can convert knowledge through action into the promised value for the customer. Defining the proficiency threshold is the crucial action for an organization to execute on its competitive strategy.

Let's take one possible promise to customers in the product and service category as an example: "Order by noon and receive your product the next day." Assuming that the fast turnaround strategy of a company in this market is correct and the value proposition will set the company apart from the competition, the leaders can now look directly at the proficiency threshold needed by the workforce to deliver on this promise. The easiest way to do this is to clearly understand the specific process within the organization that creates value for a customer. Linking the steps of this process builds what is known as the value chain. In this example, the value chain has four significant links, shown in Figure 3.5. Each of these functions in the company will be involved in delivering on this promise to customers.

Starting with the proposition of fast turnaround (order by noon and receive products the next day), the proficiency threshold for each link of the value chain can now be clearly identified. One of the biggest advantages with this approach is that it allows workers to understand how their proficiency will deliver value to

Order by noon and receive your products the next day

Procurement, Inventory Management	Sales, Marketing, Customer Service	Shipping, Packaging	Technical Support and Service

FIGURE 3.5. The Value Chain.

the customer and build barriers for the competition. The relationship between the value proposition, the customer, and the worker becomes abundantly clear.

Table 3.1 illustrates the performance requirements and proficiency threshold definitions for each link in this value chain. The organizational proficiency threshold is reached by having proficient workers throughout the delivery process. A weak link will result in the delivery of a potentially weak product or service. In this example, decision makers need to assess the individual value proposition and its importance to the overall business strategy. Taking the time to lay out the threshold definitions for this proposition will, in essence, force a set of priorities on the leaders. The organizational proficiency threshold required to make sure a customer can "order by noon and receive products the next day" can seem daunting. And this proposition is only one of ten made to customers through the company's marketing and sales efforts. The number of value propositions this organization can deliver to the marketplace—and how fast it can do this—is a function of its proficiency and the clarity of its business strategy.

Obviously, focusing on only one value proposition highlights a narrow view of the actual threshold requirements for a worker

TABLE 3.1. The Value Chain and Threshold Proficiency.

Value Proposition: Order by Noon and Receive Your Products the Next Day

Links in the Value Chain — Steps in the Process of Delivering on the Promise	Performance Requirement — What Must Be Accomplished to Deliver on the Promise	Threshold Proficiency — Initial Level of Proficiency at Which the Worker Can Deliver on the Promise
Procurement	Available inventory	*Buyer/Procurement Specialist*
Inventory Management	Accurate inventory management systems	*Literacy* Customer ordering process
		Marketing events and activity
		Shipping and packaging methods
		Fluency Usage of Inventory Management System
		Purchasing process/guidelines
		Quality assurance and warranty feedback system
Sales	Precise order placement	*Sales and Service Representative*
Marketing		*Literacy* Shipping and packaging process
Customer Service		*Fluency* Active listening
Toll-free support system		Order fulfillment system/product selection, service and pricing
		Inventory Management System

Links in the Value Chain Steps in the Process of Delivering on the Promise	Performance Requirement What Must Be Accomplished to Deliver on the Promise	Threshold Proficiency Initial Level of Proficiency at Which the Worker Can Deliver on the Promise
Shipping and Packaging	Accurate inventory management system Efficient warehouse retrieval process High-quality and efficient packaging process Quick turnaround with overnight delivery company	*Warehouse and Packaging Specialist* *Literacy* Order Fulfillment System *Fluency* Inventory Management System Warehouse automated retrieval system (part numbering scheme) Packaging quality standards and process Delivery process with UPS, FedEx, Airborne
Technical Service and Support	Development of specific packaging and shipping requirements and instructions	*Technical Service Representative* *Literacy* Order Fulfillment System *Fluency* Vendor technical requirements (storage and packaging) Customer feedback and complaints (unpacking)

in this value chain. Examining the sum of the requirements for meeting each of the propositions throughout the delivery process reveals the proficiency requirements for the entire organization and for all workers in that organization. You can see the beginning of this analysis for this company in Table 3.1. Each worker will then know the definition of his or her minimal proficiency requirements in the three categories of value delivery. This understanding, for both the worker and the decision maker, creates a momentum of learning activity that is directed toward the customer. Any training event outside this target will slow the speed with which the worker can become proficient enough to provide value to the customer.

Threshold Proficiency and the Back Office

Every position in an organization provides value to customers—even supporting personnel through their interactions with "internal customers." Quick turnaround of action items and project commitments, thorough research, well-tested designs, and accurate data are all examples of the value propositions that employees give to each other every day in the operation of a business. These are crucial to the success of any operation and should be treated just like value propositions to customers in terms of threshold proficiency.

This strategy is consistent with W. Edwards Deming's notion that in internal customer-supplier relationships, the next person in the process should be treated as a customer.[2] Deming wrote at length about the importance of never passing along a defect to a fellow employee, because it will obstruct the next step in the process and will eventually find its way to the customer. The defect in this case could be slow and unresponsive service, dated information, or high labor costs. Each component in the value chain must increase customer value, not subtract from it. In most cases, every department, from the finance department to facilities management to industrial engineering and information technologies support groups, have a sweeping impact on the value chain. This is why a definition of internal threshold levels of proficiency must be developed.

> By definition, the proficiency threshold links an individual worker to the vision and strategy of the organization in the context of his or her performance.

A worker who supplies value to the internal processes must have the same understanding of the business strategy and value proposition as a worker who directly affects the delivery of a product or service to an external customer. It is essential that support staff understand their own contributions to the final value delivered to a customer. They then perceive themselves as instrumental in the overall vision and mission of the company. Organizations that have developed proficiency threshold targets for support workers find that the method for developing them is itself a key tool for revealing the definition of value among support staff, who are usually far removed from the actual delivery to customers. Figure 3.6 illustrates one internal value proposition for the cost management group of a midsized software development company in San Jose, California. It identifies for this company the specific value propositions in Kaplan and Norton's three categories: product and service, image, and relationship.

Product
and Service $\Big\{$ *Accurate weekly cost reports*
Accurate monthly operations report (actual to budget)

Image $\Big\{$ *Smart and competent financial managers*

Relationship $\Big\{$ *Quick turnaround; responsive and easy to work with*

FIGURE 3.6. Internal Value Proposition.

As with the external value chain, the components of an internal value chain need to be described. In this case, the proposed value of an accurate monthly report is deemed crucial: an erroneous report could have serious consequences for the business and negatively affect the external value chain leading to the customer. Therefore, the individuals producing the needed report must reach threshold proficiency quickly. The components of the chain are shown in Figure 3.7.

Many support roles are performed by small groups of workers and often by a single person. In this example, the way the internal value chain is defined relative to the internal value proposition defines the proficiency threshold not only for the cost management group but also for a single worker in that group. This definition of the value chain gives each worker an understanding of the proficiency requirements to deliver on the service. Consider the operational advantages of having a support worker linked to the rest of the business through a clear definition of what must be delivered and how much know-how is required to deliver it. Table 3.2 (pp. 58–59) lays out the performance requirements and threshold proficiency definition for this cost management team.

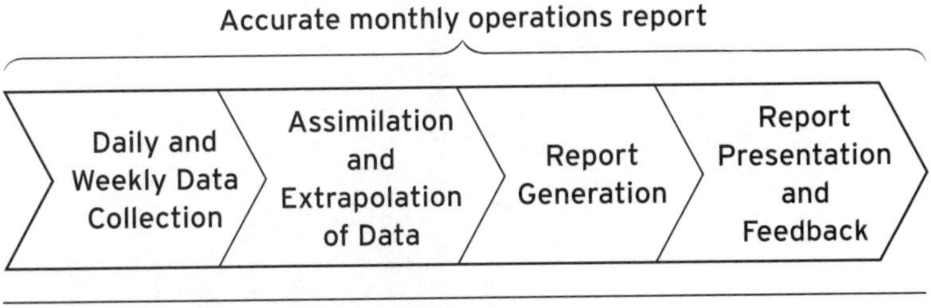

Accurate monthly operations report

```
╱‾‾‾‾‾‾‾‾‾‾‾‾‾‾‾‾‾‾‾‾‾‾‾‾‾‾‾‾‾╲‾‾‾‾‾‾‾‾‾‾‾‾‾‾‾‾‾‾‾‾‾‾‾‾‾‾‾‾
```

| Daily and Weekly Data Collection | Assimilation and Extrapolation of Data | Report Generation | Report Presentation and Feedback |

FIGURE 3.7. Internal Value Chain.

Initiating the Breakaway

Delivering value to customers rapidly is made possible by building the basic capacity of an organization and its people to get their jobs done more quickly and effectively—to reach threshold levels of proficiency fast. A breakaway starts when you reach the proficiency threshold. Proficient workers become contributing team members, they produce innovative ideas, they work safely but quickly, they go on to achieve even greater levels of proficiency, and they win the race.

TABLE 3.2. The Internal Value Chain and Threshold Proficiency.
Value Proposition: Accurate Monthly Operations Report

Links in the Value Chain Steps in the Process of Delivering on the Promise	Performance Requirement What Must Be Accomplished to Deliver on the Promise	Threshold Proficiency Initial Level of Proficiency at Which the Worker Can Deliver on the Promise
Daily and weekly data collection	Accurate collection process Timely collection method Collecting the correct data	*Cost Manager* *Literacy* Data collection procedures within the business processes *Fluency* Usage of Cost Management System Labor collection, Payables, Expenses Inventory Control, Contract Management
Assimilation and extrapolation of the data	Ensure that costs are allocated to the proper cost center, billed to the correct project and in the correct billing period Analyze the causes for deviations from the forecast	*Cost Manager* *Fluency* Cost allocation and billing codes Forecast and operating assumptions Performance metrics *Mastery* Operational analysis of cost overruns

Links in the Value Chain Steps in the Process of Delivering on the Promise	Performance Requirement What Must Be Accomplished to Deliver on the Promise	Threshold Proficiency Initial Level of Proficiency at Which the Worker Can Deliver on the Promise
	Check current operating assumptions with actual performance and suggest changes	
Report generation	Development of an accurate and brief cost management report for the operation	*Cost Manager* *Fluency* Report and presentation guidelines PowerPoint software Expectations of senior management

CHAPTER FOUR

Rule 2: Accelerate the Accumulation of Experience

> The accumulation of experience is by far the most critical step in the learning process, yet the management of and investment in this phase is nearly always left to chance.

On a recent trip, I happened to be standing on the airport escalator behind a woman who was schlepping what seemed like enough luggage for four people. Coincidentally, she was seated next to me on the flight. She had been forced to check her largest bag but was adamant about carrying on three others and crowding them under the seats—hers and mine—and in the overhead compartment.

During the flight, she pulled out four bulging three-ring binders. For nearly an hour, she wrestled with the binders, placing sticky notes on specific pages and jotting down reminders in the text. As our conversation developed, she explained that she was bound for New Jersey to facilitate a weeklong sales training class for her company.

"What do you expect out of your students after they attend the class?" I asked her. As if on cue, she turned to a tab in one of the binders, clipped open the rings, and handed me five neatly outlined sheets, each labeled "Learning Outcomes." There was one outline for every day of her course. It seemed to make sense until I looked closely at the outlines. Stuffed into five eight-hour training sessions was what must have been enough information for a full semester of a college marketing course. In one forty-hour training session, she would try to jam massive amounts of information into the brains of her students.

This was a classic example of contemporary corporate training—all things delivered in one session. Condensed schedules have forced designers to cram as much material and information as possible into the available time period, a reactive management response to perceived needs. Corporate educators usually have only one chance to work with their students, and they try to get through the greatest amount of material in the time they have. The facilitator's plight forced me to reexamine my own thinking and the logic behind the current corporate training model. I began to realize that the model fails to reflect how people really learn. In particular, it denies the most critical phase of learning—the accumulation of experience.

How People Really Learn

Every day, thousands of employees from around the country are sent to similar five-day training seminars in sales processes like the one my travel companion was facilitating. The decision to send them assumes that all of them are at ground zero in their familiarity with the new concepts. And because nothing is planned to reinforce the information conveyed in the class once they are back on the job, it is additionally assumed that they will automatically be better, more productive salespeople immediately following the training. Even more far-fetched is the assumption that salespeople will gladly give up five days of potential commissions because they seek the benefits that will result from taking the class. These misguided and false training assumptions become an enormous obstacle to the organization's ability to learn faster—indeed, they may prevent employees from learning anything at all.

It is time to use the past century's research on human learning to understand how we have strayed and to find our path to the future. We know from more than nine decades of research that adults do not learn without a natural progression from discovery through experience. Three thinkers in particular have informed our understanding of this fact.

John Dewey, an educator born during the Civil War, was truly one of the pioneers of inquiry into human thought and learning. His research at the University of Chicago and later at Columbia University is the seminal work on the human as a learner and a performer. His book *How We Think*, published in 1910, serves as a springboard for understanding the training of the human mind.

Dewey draws a strong distinction between the *acquisition of* information and the *application of* practice *and* thinking, the latter being the only true way for a human to learn. "There is all the difference in the world when the acquisition of information is treated as an end in itself, or is made an integral portion of the training of thought. *The assumption that information which has been accumulated apart from the use in the recognition and solution of a problem may later on be freely employed at will by thought is quite false.*"[1]

Dewey continues, "The skill acquired with the aid of intelligence, the only information which, otherwise than by accident, can be put to logical use, is that acquired in the course of think-ing while experiencing. Because their knowledge has been achieved in connection with the needs of specific situations, men of little book-learning are often able to put to effective use every ounce of knowledge they possess; while men of vast erudi-tion are often swamped by the mere bulk of their learning, because memory, rather than experience, has been the operative in obtaining it."[2]

Another researcher who has contributed greatly to the under-standing of human learning is Robert Gagné, arguably the fore-father of instructional design. During his five decades of research, Gagné produced a framework for linking human learning with a process for instruction. Table 4.1, adapted from a paper he pub-lished in 1970, highlights this relationship.[3]

Gagné contended that instruction must be integrated with four natural learning processes. The *introductory phase* sets the stage for learning by engaging the student's interest and atten-tion. The *initial guidance phase* supports the initial learning by giving directions, suggestions, and prompts. The *application*

TABLE 4.1. Learning Processes and Phases of Instruction.

Phase of Instruction	Phase of Proficiency	Learning Process
Introductory phase	Introduction	Motivation, attention, selective perception
Initial guidance phase	Assimilation	Coding, storage entry
Application phase	Translation	Retention, retrieval, transfer
Performance and feedback phase	Accumulation	Performance, reinforcement

phase is directed at retrieval, with the aim of retention. And finally, the *performance and feedback phase* is targeted at creating situations for student performance by providing feedback relevant to that performance. Gagné's work holds that learners progress through all four learning processes on their way to achieving a new level of performance; if instruction is intended to advance a learner's performance, it must be designed to take a learner all the way to the fourth phase, performance and feedback.

Finally, the recent work of John R. Anderson on the integration of learning and memory divides how skills develop into three stages, using as an example the act of learning how to shift gears with a manual transmission.[4] In the initial act of learning, called the *cognitive stage,* the learner works from a set of instructions or observations. A student driver, for example, is exposed to the principles of a standard transmission and sees a demonstration. In the second stage, called the *associative stage,* the skill makes a transition from a declaration to a procedure. The learner in this stage begins to experiment with the instructions. For instance, the student driver learns to coordinate the releasing of the clutch with the application of the gas pedal so as to not kill the engine. Finally, a learner progresses to the *autonomous stage,* where the skill becomes repeated in an automated and rapid fashion. In this stage, cognitive involvement is gradually eliminated—it becomes second nature. Most drivers advancing to this stage do not even realize a separate relationship between the clutch, the gas pedal, and the stick shift. Anderson concludes that as a skill becomes more practiced, it undergoes dramatic changes, including great reductions in its cognitive involvement; hence improved performance requires a learner to reach the autonomous stage.

The Four Phases of Learning

These thinkers have contributed greatly to the understanding of learning and the human mind. Sadly, few of their conclusions are known and applied consistently outside of academia. To build a bridge between this landmark research and the daily challenges of business leaders, I have attempted to relate these key principles and theories to the everyday practice and language of today's business environment. During the course of research for this book, I observed companies creating new learning for workers to reach the proficiency threshold and deliver value to customers fast. I identified four phases in this real-world learning process, culminating in the accumulation of experience and increased performance:

1. *Introduction* to new information

2. *Assimilation* of the newly acquired information with previous knowledge and experience

3. *Translation* of the new information combined with past experience into specific knowledge

4. *Accumulation* of experience through practice, trial and error, and feedback on performance

Let's look at these in greater detail. The first phase requires the *introduction* of new information. The learner must be exposed to a new set of data to initiate the process. Information comes to us in an endless variety of forms and through a myriad of media every day. Capturing the learner's attention requires that this information be new and different. In the training process I am describing, this phase is finished in a very short period of time.

> We know from more than nine decades of research that adults do not learn without a natural progression from discovery through experience.

In the second phase, the learner *assimilates* the new data, combining them with previous knowledge and experience. It is during this phase that a learner passes judgment about whether the new information or potential new skill has real benefit. The learner asks, "What's in it for me?" and the answer either activates or suppresses interest in learning.

Few people can both consume new information *and* change their performance or behavior immediately. So in the third phase, learners reflect on the new information and *translate* it into the world in which they work—to place the information in the context of their jobs and thus to understand how it fits. Without going through the process of translation, a learner is merely "informed" and can rarely make the leap to any form of application or practice.

Let's pause to reflect on these three stages. At this point, the prospective learner is versed in and has contextual knowledge of the subject matter. In the industry vernacular, "training and development" is the sum of phase 1 and phase 2 and occasionally part of phase 3. In other words, once they have gone this far, learners in traditional training are assumed to have been "trained." Evaluations of well-designed training sessions include such questions as "Will the information gained from this course help you perform better in your job?" and "As a result of this course, can you better describe why we need to continually improve the service to our customers?" Good scores or positive answers to these questions lead one to believe that the training has been effective, but training by this definition is only a fraction of the learning process.

That's because the most important learning occurs in the fourth and most time-consuming phase, when knowledge is transformed into practice through an *accumulation* of experience using the new knowledge. The learning is not complete until experience is accumulated and the proficiency threshold is reached. *The accumulation of experience is by far the most critical step in the learning process, yet the management of and investment in this phase is nearly always left to chance.* Although the accumulation of experience requires time and resources many times greater than those required for the first three phases, these resources are rarely budgeted, and the accumulation of experience generally occurs by accident, not design.

It is crucial that we grasp the implications of this oversight. If the accumulation of experience is not managed, it does still occur on the job, but it costs much more in time and money than if it had been designed. The costs are reflected in lost sales, lost customers, employee turnover, overtime, accidents, scrap and rework, and disappointing improvements in productivity.

Accumulation of Experience Left to Chance

An example from the telecommunications industry will help drive home this point. The Internet revolution has been made possible by the conversion of our communications infrastructure from copper wire to fiber-optic cables made of long, narrow strands of glass. The telecommunications industry has an aching shortage of workers who can connect, or *splice,* these glass cables. Across the country, fiber-optic cables sit, waiting to be spliced; the lack of skilled workers has become a significant bottleneck in the conversion process. In the new world of telecommunications, this shortage alone can be responsible for a company's failure to compete, while the companies that get their workers to proficiency fast will enjoy an enormous advantage against their competition.

It typically takes eight weeks—forty working days—for an experienced copper splicer to become proficient at splicing glass cables. The training begins with a classroom lecture from an instructor who *introduces* the differences between copper and glass splicing, the placement of the fiber cable, the engineering requirements for quality of the connection and conductivity, and the special safety requirements for working with microscopic glass. The student *assimilates* the new information with previous experience splicing copper wire. At the end of the first week, the classroom information is placed into a three-ring binder and carried into the next week's lab work, in which for three days the learner uses the precision tools required to laser-weld two extremely thin pieces of glass together. In this phase, the learner goes from being a copper splicer who twists two pieces of wire together with a nut to a fiber-optic splicer who uses sophisticated tools to connect glass strands. The new information and past experience are *translated* into new knowledge.

In a questionnaire submitted at the end of the class, typically more than 90 percent of the students claim that they have enough new knowledge and know-how to splice fiber-optic cable. But the truth is that these workers aren't yet ready to deliver on the promise made to customers. Up to this point, workers have learned in a controlled environment. Following the class, however, some are needed for other work and are not available for splicing work for a number of weeks; their road to proficiency is difficult because of memory decay following the class. Those who go directly to work in splicing jobs encounter all sorts of new situations—deep, muddy excavations; water-filled service holes; broken cable that is fractured at random points, contaminated with dirt, or otherwise touched by Mother Nature in ways not anticipated in the classroom. The learner must adapt classroom knowledge to the real problems found in the field. At this point, and only at this point, does a worker even *begin* to cross the bridge to the proficiency threshold by *accumulating experience* with the new knowledge.

> The traditional training model ignores completely the need for learners to accumulate experience, and accumulation therefore proceeds at its own pace, generally driven by various emergencies.

From the start of training, it took an average of eight weeks before the worker could deliver on the promise to customers. Of these eight weeks, only the first two were budgeted, managed, designed, and measured (see Figure 4.1). In the following six weeks, the worker's attempt to gain enough experience to splice fiber optics was not only left to chance but was also fraught with

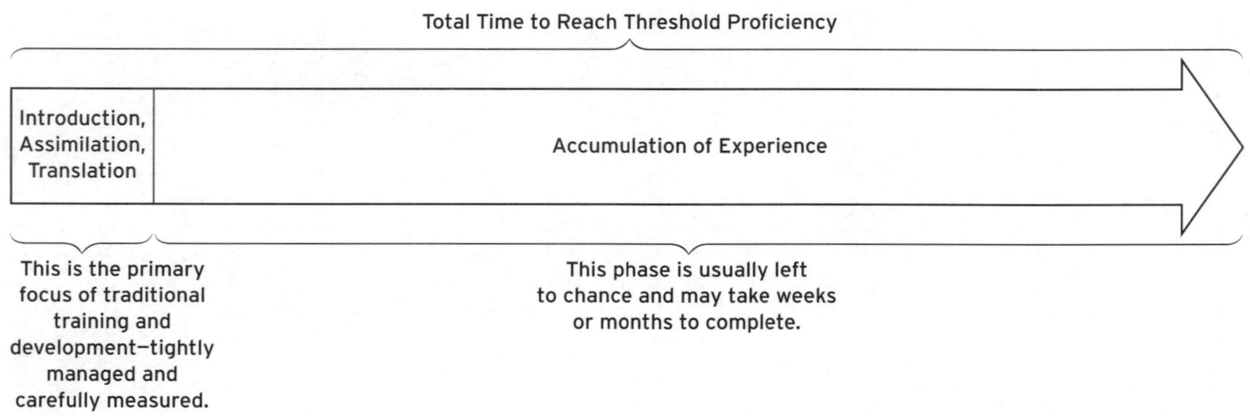

Total Time to Reach Threshold Proficiency

Accumulation of Experience

Introduction, Assimilation, Translation

This is the primary focus of traditional training and development—tightly managed and carefully measured.

This phase is usually left to chance and may take weeks or months to complete.

FIGURE 4.1. Learning Process in Traditional Training and Development.

potential inconsistencies and bad habits formed through the random learning process.

The traditional training model assumes that at the end of a training event, a worker will immediately have the knowledge and ability to perform more effectively. It ignores completely the need for learners to accumulate experience, and accumulation therefore proceeds at its own pace, generally driven by various emergencies. Some employees never reach proficiency; others achieve it only through trial and error, practicing on real customers.

Managing the Accumulation of Experience

What if an organization could dramatically reduce the time it took its employees to reach threshold proficiency by managing the accumulation of experience instead of leaving it to chance? What if an organization could get its workers to the point where they could meet customers' needs much faster than the competition?

Fortunately, there is an approach that differs radically from traditional training and development practice, one that offers organizations huge competitive advantages. In the case of the telecommunications firm discussed earlier, the approach allowed it to train workers to splice fiber-optic cables in an average of three weeks instead of eight. By managing the accumulation of experience and the rate at which it occurs, this organization dramatically reduced the time it took to create proficient employees and deliver value to its customers.

Here's how the company did it. The organization decided that after the classroom training, the expert training instructors would accompany their students into the field. Their new role as field coaches: to go on the job with a group of six workers and coach them until each could splice an entire cable of 144 hair-thin fiber-optic lines unassisted. When all six employees have passed this test, the instructors receive another group of six learners. "I traded my wingtips for boots, and it changed my life overnight," one coach said.

The field learning followed a classic model: the expert would demonstrate splicing under real-world conditions, with the learners watching and asking questions. Then the learners would splice, and the expert would provide immediate, personalized feedback. Learning and work were made one and the same. A majority of the training budget was redirected to the accumulation of experience, enabling workers to reach threshold proficiency in three weeks instead of eight and greatly increasing the organization's capacity to meet customers' needs. Figure 4.2 illustrates this change in approach.

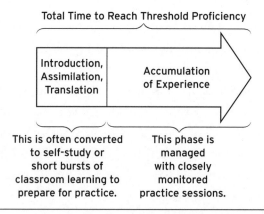

FIGURE 4.2. Learning Process When the Focus Is on Accelerating the Accumulation of Experience.

In the end, it is the accumulation of experience that affords the most opportunity to reduce the cycle time it takes to become proficient and to gain significant competitive advantage. Managing the rapid accumulation of experience offers the biggest opportunity to shorten the cycle time to proficiency, period.

To sum up so far: breakaway training and development begins with defining the value propositions for your organization. Next, establish proficiency thresholds for the core tasks for each job, keeping in mind that different jobs require different levels of proficiency for different tasks. Using the proficiency thresholds as the defined outcomes of training and development experiences, design the training to shorten the time devoted to introduction, assimilation, and translation, and make explicit provisions for managing the accelerated accumulation of experience. At this point, you are well on your way to creating a breakaway. The next step, discussed in Chapter Five, is to measure your success.

CHAPTER FIVE

Rule 3: Measure the Cycle Time to Threshold Proficiency

Cycle time to threshold proficiency is a metric that will

fundamentally change the planning, budgeting, and behavior

of the individuals charged with the overall competence of an

organization's workforce.

In the early 1980s, I worked for a seasoned supervisor who also moonlighted as an industrial engineering professor at a local community college. As one might imagine, he was nuts about process measurement and statistical process control. His favorite mantra was "What gets measured gets done." He didn't originate the phrase, of course, but he was clearly someone who understood the relationship of process to measurement and worker behavior. I have come to appreciate the wisdom in his teaching for the success or failure of learning programs. This chapter presents a powerful alternative to traditional training metrics, one that is directly related to achieving proficiency and delivering value to customers faster.

Take the proverbial "butts in seats" measurement of training practiced by many organizations. This metric drives the training manager to build and maintain elaborate scheduling systems for routing workers into classes. It directs instructional designers to think in terms of "instructional days" and encourages savvy workers to build up a mountain of hours in their training transcripts. In turn, decision makers, witnessing more workers completing more hours of training, become complacent in their judgment of the education system and assume that it is working. Ironically, most would agree that the number of people attending a course has little relationship to how well they ultimately perform on the job, yet many organizations continue to use training hours as the ultimate metric for success or failure of learning programs.

A New Metric of Human Development

To increase the speed by which an organization can deliver on its value proposition, a new measure and a new perspective are needed. *Cycle time to threshold proficiency* is a metric that will fundamentally change the planning, budgeting, and behavior of individuals charged with the overall competence of an organization's workforce.

Cycle time to threshold proficiency, unlike butts in seats, is a measurement that is consistent with business practice that is already used across nearly all parts of an organization aside from the training department. If the beginning and end points of a process can be defined and a clock or calendar is available, cycle time can be measured. Wasteful steps hidden in the daily operational system become illuminated when the objective of training is not to fill seats or produce instructional days but rather to reduce the amount of time it takes each worker to become proficient and perform.[1] It is for this reason that improvements in execution speed follow cycle time measurement. Remember, "What gets measured gets done."

Measuring cycle time to threshold proficiency means measuring the process that occurs as a worker accumulates enough experience to provide value to the customer. The overall measure of cycle time to proficiency takes into account all time between the first learning event and the ultimate performance. Figure 5.1 illustrates the cycle time to threshold proficiency in a typical example of traditional training and development. After the initial learning event in which the worker goes through the process of introduction, assimilation, and translation of new material, the critical accumulation of experience is left to chance, and therefore the entire process of reaching the proficiency threshold may take six months or more.

As one can see, the proficiency threshold metric differs greatly from the standard practice of measuring a single event—such as three-day classroom training—within the larger process. The key difference is that it measures the total time it takes for an individual to achieve the desired level of performance so that value can be delivered to customers.

This insight drives the decision makers of the organization to focus on steps in the learning process that will most dramatically reduce the overall cycle time. In the example in Figure 5.1, this is neither the 3-day course nor the 13 days it takes for workers to complete all of the traditional training but rather the 180 days needed to accumulate the experience necessary to perform at the threshold level. The cycle time to proficiency metric provides a panoramic view of a worker's path toward performance, producing the data needed to identify the resources that will quicken the pace. An astute leader, using our example, would focus on the accumulation of experience phase, as it represents over 90 percent of the cycle time and the biggest area for improvement.

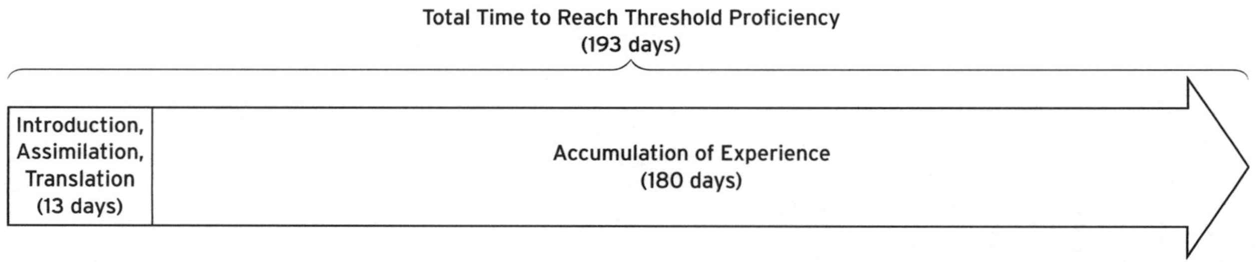

Total Time to Reach Threshold Proficiency
(193 days)

Introduction, Assimilation, Translation (13 days)

Accumulation of Experience (180 days)

FIGURE 5.1. Cycle Time in Traditional Training and Development.

Many corporations around the globe are trying to reduce the time a worker spends in the classroom or attending a training event. If you seek a clear operational advantage, redirect your focus from further compressing the introduction, assimilation, and translation events and instead apply innovation and resources to the accumulation of experience. Figure 5.2 shows that by accelerating the accumulation of experience, an organization can cut the cycle time to proficiency by two-thirds, saving more than one hundred days per employee. This clearly outweighs the extreme effort required to reduce a three-day course to two days—a course that will still leave performers well short of the proficiency threshold.

Measuring the Proficiency Rate

In addition to measuring cycle time to proficiency for individuals, an organization must measure its proficiency rate—the speed with which the organization is able to deliver on a partic-

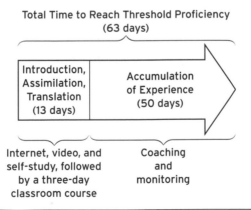

FIGURE 5.2. Cycle Time When the Focus Is on the Accumulation of Experience.

ular value proposition. Hours-in-class metrics consider only size of population and so offer no basis for competitive comparison, forecasting, or improvement. Nor can *individual* cycle time help organizations understand the complexities added, for example, when sheer numbers of people or limitations of infrastructure require that training take place in smaller groups, or *flights*, over an extended period of time. Linking the average cycle time of individuals reaching proficiency with the total number of people needed to reach the threshold level will enable a leader to measure and monitor the speed at which the organization is learning in order to deliver on a specific promise to customers.

This measurement is a kind of velocity, except that instead of being expressed in miles per hour or feet per second, this measurement of speed is expressed in terms of the number of people reaching the proficiency threshold in a defined period of time. The proficiency rate allows us to see learning not as simply a required event with no direct, measurable connection to the value proposition but rather as a concrete, operational measure of business efficiency. The proficiency rate thus gives leaders flexibility because they can use it to make real-time decisions quickly. Both the effectiveness and the efficiency of training are measured with this new thinking, as shown in Table 5.1.

> The proficiency rate allows us to see learning not as a compulsory event with no direct, measurable connection to the value proposition but rather as a concrete, operational measure of business efficiency.

TABLE 5.1. Proficiency Rate Versus Traditional Quality Metrics.

Traditional Measures	New Proficiency Metrics
Effectiveness	
Number of people in class	Number of people working to deliver on the value proposition
Number of total training hours	Cycle time to reach threshold proficiency
Efficiency	
Total training hours per person per year	Proficiency rate: number of workers achieving threshold proficiency per day

---

An organization's proficiency rate is calculated by taking the number of employees attempting to reach threshold proficiency and dividing this number by the average cycle time to proficiency of workers reaching the threshold level:

$$\text{organizational proficiency rate} = \frac{\text{number of employees attempting to reach threshold proficiency}}{\text{current average cycle time to proficiency}}$$

The average is derived from a sample taken at strategic intervals as flights of targeted workers continue down the developmental path. The result is a unit of proficiency for the entire group over time—the number of proficient workers produced per day. Typical measurement intervals are weekly and often include an assessment, on-the-job performance criteria, and client feedback. Leaders can watch for overall improvement and trends that indicate that the accumulation of experience is improving as flights of workers complete training and more workers reach the threshold level. The power of this metric comes not only from its simplicity but also from its ability to help leaders understand the *rate at which their organization is changing*. It is clearly not an absolute measure but rather an indicator of how fast learners are reaching the proficiency threshold for a specific effort to deliver value to customers. Each effort will have a different rate as the number of people needed and the complexity of the task change with each journey toward threshold proficiency.

To illustrate the proficiency rate with an example, let's turn to a global communications provider currently undertaking the daunting task of training customer service representatives to provide the company's new connection services. Each representative must be able to receive a customer call, discover which PCS device (phone, pager, and so on) the customer has purchased, and establish the new service within a given time period, all while the customer remains on the line—this is the company's value proposition. Each week, thirty-five employees are grouped into a new flight and begin the process toward threshold proficiency. Each representative practices on a simulator, completes online product and information courses, and practices with other employees in the flight before completing a series of customer conversations aided by a coach in order to establish the connection successfully for the customer.

Table 5.2 indicates the progress this company has made toward having its employees reach proficiency quickly. When this program was begun, the average cycle time to threshold proficiency was twelve days. Some employees would reach the

TABLE 5.2. The Proficiency Rate in Action.

Week	Employees per Flight	Average Cycle Time to Proficiency (days)	Proficiency Rate[a]	Improvement in Proficiency Rate	Total Workers Reaching Proficiency[b]
2	35	12	2.9	0%	35
5	35	9.4	3.7	28%	140
10	35	7.7	4.5	55%	318
15	35	6.3	5.6	94%	482

[a] proficient workers created per day
[b] excluding turnover

threshold in just a few days, and others were taking up to twenty days. The average at twelve days netted a proficiency rate of 2.9, calculated by dividing the thirty-five employees by the group's average cycle time to proficiency. Over the next fifteen weeks, nearly five hundred employees went through the program, the management team implemented a number of improvements to the simulator, and the coaches became more efficient. At week 15, the proficiency rate was 5.6. "What is most important to us is that we become faster over time," the manager says. "We reduced the cycle time to proficiency by 50 percent for each flight of employees, but if you look at the proficiency rate, we were reaching proficiency as a group nearly 100 percent faster than when we started this effort!"

Revisiting the Learning Curve

The concept of proficiency rate enables a better understanding of the commonly misunderstood notion of the learning curve.

Although the term *learning curve* is often used by people discussing training, I am surprised by how poorly understood it is. In a recent presentation at an American Society for Training and Development conference, for example, a speaker kept referring to the "steep" learning curve in his organization. His implications of a tough climb and difficult individual battles with learning, however, showed how little he understood the concept: contrary to common usage, the steeper the learning curve, the faster and more efficient the learning. Once understood, this tool will help leaders make better and more timely decisions regarding the development of their people.

Learning curves were first employed in the airframe industry to forecast the labor savings that resulted from the accumulated experience of building one airframe after another. In essence, the technique links unit costs with volume and presumes that as cumulative unit volume increases, learning occurs, and the costs per unit decline.[2]

Three key assumptions are used in learning curve theory:

- The amount of time required to complete a given task will be less each time the task is undertaken.

- Unit time will decrease at a decreasing rate.

- The reduction in unit time will follow a predictable pattern.[3]

The airframe industry refined the theory to a relatively precise science using data from each successive performance. For example, if the assembly of aircraft 1 required one hundred thousand hours of labor; aircraft 2, eighty thousand hours; aircraft 3, sixty-four thousand hours; and so on, the organization is experiencing a 20 percent reduction in required labor following the assembly of each plane. This is considered an 80 percent learning curve. Note that the lower the percentage, the faster the learning.

The economies of the learning curve are realized through changes in learning rates and can have a dramatic effect on a company's overall competitiveness. As shown in Figure 5.3, being able to learn only 5 percent faster can deliver a direct blow to a slower-learning competitor. In this hypothetical case, a company with a learning curve of 85 percent has a cost-per-unit advantage of $13 (13 percent) over a company with a learning curve of 90 percent, directly attributable to reduction in required labor. The stark truth communicated through the learning curve is that proficiency and performance cannot be faked: the cost per unit improves only when output increases or input decreases.

The number of units produced over a period of time can also

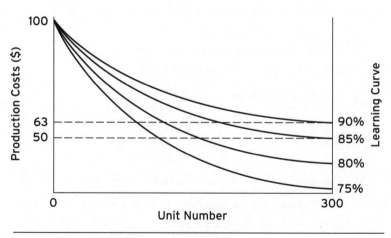

FIGURE 5.3. Comparison of Learning Curves.

be represented using the learning curve. This displays learning as a function of time rather than decreases in unit cost and thus provides for a direct link to the cycle time to threshold proficiency. Figure 5.4 represents the learning curve in units per day over time. As in Figure 5.3, notice that the "steepest" curve actually indicates the fastest and most efficient learning.

Financial analysts in manufacturing have traditionally been the biggest users of the learning curve, but don't be fooled by its manufacturing roots. Excuses for not using it in service industries include the elusive definition of a unit of service and the short life cycles of services. Take, for example, one of the many business offerings now available that are customized for each customer, such as in financial services. One could argue that a learning curve could not measure a customized service because the unit volume is only one. In fact, the opposite is true. Remember, the learning curve compares the cost components of a well-defined

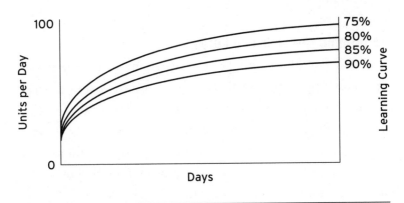

FIGURE 5.4. Learning Curve Represented in Units per Day.

process against the experience or competence needed to successfully complete the steps within that particular process. The key to measuring productivity for service providers lies in identifying the knowledge and experience at the lowest level of detail, standardizing as many details as possible, and combining and mixing the details at the point of contact with the customer. World-class service providers know precisely the amount of time and cost required for each unit of service. ServiceMaster, for example, measures each unit of maintenance work; McDonald's, each unit of food preparation; Qwest, each telephone response; and United Parcel Service, each package delivered. These small and replicable units are the keys to effective capacity planning, work assignment, customer service, and competitive differentiation.[4] Therefore, learning curve methodology applies to service organizations even more than to manufacturers. In a manufacturing system, it may take months to complete enough units to plot the learning curve. In a service environment, thousands of service units are produced daily, enabling a near-instant metric for learning.

Redefining the Learning Curve

Unfortunately, the learning curve is rarely applied in the emerging knowledge economy. Becoming the lowest-cost or highest-volume producer is only one dimension in an economy based on information, quality, and speed. Being the lowest-cost, lowest-priced producer may actually leave a company open for ambush by a competitor who can offer an equivalent product or service with more speed. Consumers continually remind us that they are willing to pay for speed. And a single-minded focus on unit cost reduction might lead some decision makers to substitute capital improvements for people.[5]

A powerful competitive metric therefore comes from predicting not only the unit costs over time but also the time needed to get the organization to the point where it can deliver on the value proposition. The decision-making leverage behind a more contemporary learning curve stems from the combination of the three human-dependent variables—quality, cycle time to proficiency, and cost. This new learning curve, which I call the *proficiency curve,* is illustrated for a hypothetical organization in Figure 5.5.

Learning curve methodology applies to service organizations even more than to manufacturers.

Consistent quality is delivered through a reliable process that quickly places workers at the threshold level of proficiency or

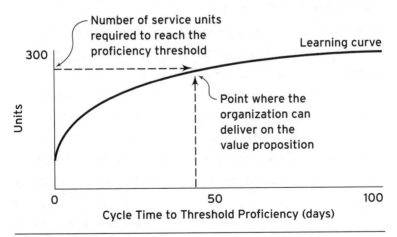

FIGURE 5.5. The Proficiency Curve.

beyond: by definition, when the organization confirms that workers are delivering the promised value to customers on the job, quality has been achieved. *Time* is defined by the customers' demand for a product or service when *they* want it—a requirement dependent on the knowledge and proficiency of employees. Organizations that have employees at the threshold level of proficiency earlier in the life cycle of a product or service (shown with a proficiency curve) can clearly compete in the time dimension—both in speed to market and in maturity and sophistication of service. *Cost* per unit of product or service is reduced as learning speed increases and the learning curve steepens, as described in Figure 5.3. Therefore, the rate by which an organization reaches the proficiency threshold dictates its ability to compete in three dimensions: quality of service, service delivery time, and overall unit cost. The proficiency curve will enable decision makers to grasp all three variables over time.

The Partners of Starbucks

Recently, while I was giving a speech to a group of investors interested in the education industry, one gentleman challenged the notion of competing with proficient workers: "Tell me of a company that actually operates in this manner," he said. Good question. Here's my answer: to understand how speed to proficiency actually works to redirect decisions regarding the development of people, we need only look to a company that most are familiar with, Starbucks. I am not only an admirer and a devout shareholder but also a frequent consumer of its services. Over the course of the past three years, I have had many interviews with the employees, or "partners," of Starbucks around the world. In

1987, Starbucks operated eleven stores and had one hundred employees. Fourteen years later, the company operates more than 3,300 retail locations and registers a 30 percent top-line improvement over the previous year. This places annual revenues at about $600 million and growing.

Howard Schultz, CEO of Starbucks and author of *Pour Your Heart into It,* has a passion for the continual proficiency of each partner in the Starbucks family. Even though nearly two-thirds of all partners are part-time employees, they are the heart and soul of the company. This stems from Schultz's understanding that "every dollar earned passes through their hands."[6] The proficiency threshold for the retail partners is a level of performance that results in superior customer service—service that will bring customers back to Starbucks. From Sydney to Toronto, each new partner clearly understands this proposition.

Each partner hired to work in a retail capacity at Starbucks receives a minimum of twenty-five hours of training during the first two to four weeks with the company. This includes substantial training in customer service skills, coffee knowledge, and drink-making techniques. As explained by a team of enthusiastic partners of a Denver Starbucks store, "We continue to practice on ourselves after the training—which is how we get really good!"[7] By the fourth week, they are fluent in the daily operational details of the store. They know how to gain the respect of customers, no matter what mood the customers are in; they can quickly create any drink on the menu within tight quality standards for temperature, texture, and flavor; and they can operate the computer cash register and explain to a customer the difference between the two major types of coffee beans and the effect roasting has on them.

Those who reach a mastery level of proficiency in these tasks—on purpose—become the mentors and teachers for the next generation of partners.

Even as retail partners are reaching their proficiency threshold, nonretail employees (for example, accountants) reach a literacy level of proficiency in retail tasks by working for a few days each quarter in a store or roasting plant. Given this level of attention to employee proficiency, perhaps we should not be surprised that Starbucks is far ahead of the competition in employee loyalty. Nationwide, retailers and fast-food chains have an annual turnover rate ranging from 150 to 400 percent per year. Turnover at the average Starbucks ranges from 60 to 65 percent per year.[8]

Many partners attribute some of this success to the unique benefits package given to nearly all part-time partners. The ability to quickly bring delight to a customer, however, is a significant part of the generous benefits package. In general, partners perceive *their* value in the overall success of Starbucks (in the terms of this book, they understand their role in delivering value to the customer) very early in their employment—in the first few weeks.

Starbucks clearly competes on the basis of the proficiency of its partners. In less than three weeks (their average cycle time to threshold proficiency), the training process produces employees who can deliver high-quality service to customers. Not only can Starbucks deliver that service very quickly, but it clearly has competitive margins based on reaching operational effectiveness and efficiency *fast*.

If you are ready and willing to compete with Starbucks, here is your benchmark: I estimate the cycle time to proficiency for a retail partner at Starbucks to be between two and three working weeks—call it thirteen days. For every group of twenty partners, Starbucks's proficiency rate is 1.5 proficient partners per day.[9] During the first few days working at Starbucks, the average person serves between eighty and one hundred customers per day, according to the energetic new partners I interviewed. Of course, this rate improves greatly over time and varies by retail location. Thus formal training augmented by coaching in the store brings a retail partner to threshold proficiency after serving approximately six hundred customers. Furthermore, each time partners repeat the cycle of making a specific drink or operating the cash register, they do so approximately 10 percent faster than the previous time, netting a 90 percent learning curve. Figure 5.6 represents the relationship of these metrics.

Compared to others in the fast-food retailing market, Starbucks has outpaced its competitors by clearly understanding the

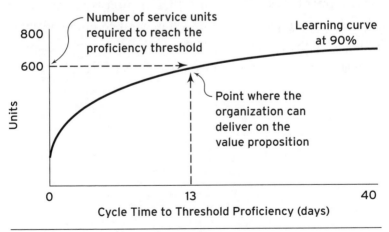

FIGURE 5.6. Starbucks's Proficiency Curve.

importance of quickly getting its partners to the threshold level of performance. While competitors (often located next door to Starbucks) struggle to retain the basic level of service, Starbucks entices its many proficient partners to organize poetry readings with customers, introduce local art and ideas, and move the "customer experience" to yet another level.

Staying Grounded

This chapter offers a new method for advancing an organization toward its competitive goals. Cycle time is a simple but powerful measurement. The learning curve is an arithmetic projection that most calculators and desktop computers can easily plot. From there it is relatively easy to figure out proficiency rates and the proficiency curve. These new metrics for speed are fundamental to changing the focus from training events to the overall process by which workers become proficient. Successful leaders will use them to modify decisions, add resources, and check regularly for improvement. Leaders will use these concepts as they were intended, as simple tools grounded in good common business sense. Keep them that way, and the result will quickly move the people of your organization forward to proficiency.

CHAPTER SIX

Putting It All Together

Orchestrating the Breakaway

Common to these organizations is a beat, a source of energy, a rhythm. These organizations seem to have discovered the difference between a single random event and a pattern of strategic activities that creates a percussive rhythm of continuous, targeted actions to promote faster learning.

W hen I began the research for this book in 1994, I was thoroughly convinced that learning and workforce proficiency were the essence of productive activity and overall competitiveness. Today, after working with more than one-third of the Fortune 50 companies and numerous mid-sized and small organizations, I am more certain than ever that this is true. I am equally certain, however, that there is no one recipe for success that is common among leading organizations. Early on, this created a serious dilemma for my research because I was truly seeking the validation of a "best practice," a standard process adhered to by companies that excelled at developing their people and competing in the marketplace.

Although there was no single best practice, I did find the specific things that produced speed to proficiency and the breakaway, as well as several themes that ran though the efforts of successful organizations as diverse as Sun Microsystems, Kinko's, ServiceMaster, and the United States Army. It is up to each company to find its own style of speed to proficiency by prioritizing among and giving concrete expression to the themes discussed in this chapter. This isn't a matter of a formula or a set of rules; it's part of the art of business. The examples in this chapter show how other companies have gone about orchestrating the breakaway.

Two Companies, Two Styles

"There is no single critical act, no step-by-step process, no matchless system for sharing information, and no formula common to organizations that learn fast." This is what I scratched on the top of my notepad during a long flight from New York to Denver. I was returning from a weeklong trip that included successful meetings with leaders at IBM and Arrow Electronics. At the time (as they are today), both companies were market leaders on a number of fronts, and both organizations had a distinct vision and strategy for the development of their workers.

At IBM, which has one of the world's largest workforces, Lou Gerstner was successfully rebuilding a company that could compete with nimble Silicon Valley competitors. The company's strategic vision was of "network-centric computing"—a world in which customers buy computing power and software applications they way they buy electric power, with the applications residing on a network that IBM owns and that businesses rent on a per-usage basis. Its value proposition was to deliver globally a unique set of skills to bring corporations painlessly into networked computing. Through a form of a "grassroots revival," the agents of change within IBM worked with a new mantra: "Rules for radicals." These leaders were given license to work on the edge—to find creative methods to immediately build a workforce that could rapidly produce and support competitive network-centric products and services.[1]

Tom Bouchard, the top human resource officer and a direct report to Gerstner, brought in Janet McAllister, a respected and seasoned operations "radical," to reinvigorate IBM's learning process. McAllister became their leader of global learning and started what has become a remarkable turnaround in the way people at IBM learn. McAllister, who now leads a successful San Francisco Bay Area Internet company, researched at length the way IBM employees prefer to learn and then built self-paced, technology-driven systems to deliver learning instantly through the Web nearly anywhere on earth. The key to IBM's use of technology is that it focused not only on the delivery of knowledge but also on practice and feedback sessions that enabled learners to take that knowledge and rapidly accumulate experience delivering value to the customer. This process included everyone in the value chain, from software engineers to sales executives. Learning speed has increased dramatically, with employees, especially new employees, able to learn at speeds only "radicals" could imagine.[2]

My second visit that week was to a very different place, Arrow Electronics, a company that continues to hold a remarkable lead in the global distribution of electronic components. This multi-billion-dollar enterprise is small in comparison to IBM but larger than life when it comes to the know-how of its workforce. Stephen Kaufman, the venerable CEO, has a strategy at the opposite pole from that of IBM. He believes in a low-tech but "high-touch" strategy for learning that technologists would call old-fashioned: his organization invests in lengthy classroom courses and extensive coaching time with subject matter experts. The process at Arrow Electronics is successful because of a relentless concentration on the learner who is attempting to reach proficiency. Very little is left to chance in the learning process as coaches and mentors assist learners from the classroom to the workspace, focused solely on getting the learner to be able to deliver value to customers in the shortest possible time. Although Arrow is just now beginning to introduce online learning, the company is miles ahead of other organizations because it already has in place a learning process that is far more powerful than technology.

Arrow Electronics is also expert at using otherwise wasted time to its advantage. For example, at its annual sales conference, which in most companies is mostly recognition and hoopla, they design simulations and practice sessions to help salespeople rapidly come up to speed on new product offerings and value propositions. When they leave the three-day conference, members of the sales force are already proficient with the new products. Kaufman considers himself and his leadership team the teachers and the ultimate role models for learning. He is one of those rare leaders who give more than lip service to the development of their people—he often personally teaches the Arrow orientation to new employees and is known for following up with people in his class a year later to see their progress. In this case, "old-fashioned" may actually be fashionable, in that Arrow may have one of the best-developed, most proficient management teams in the industry. The learning speed and operational proficiency at Arrow are proof that using technology, the Web, and self-paced learning is not the only successful approach to increasing organizational learning speed.[3]

The stark contrast between IBM's bias for technology and Arrow Electronics' traditional approach should be noted. Both companies are champions in the race to organizational proficiency, yet they use radically different methods to get ready to compete. The common denominator is that both companies truly understand the need for reaching the proficiency threshold quickly and have found creative ways to achieve this target that are consistent with their successful cultures.

Six Themes for Speed

The rules for delivering value fast that were highlighted in Chapters Three, Four, and Five govern the sequence and direction of an enterprise's plan to begin to achieve rapid rates of speed to proficiency. Momentum that will sustain and drive the improvements will come from the energy and creativity applied to the rules. There are organizations today that have reduced the cycle time to proficiency for a specific skill by as much as 80 percent. Common to these organizations is a beat, a source of energy, a rhythm. These organizations seem to have discovered the difference between a single random event and a pattern of strategic activities that creates a percussive rhythm of continuous, targeted actions to promote faster learning. When witnessing one of these organizations in action, one finds a relentless source of personal and operational energy directed at consuming new knowledge, learning, and performing.

This source of energy, this rhythm, is often strikingly different from one company to the next, but a similar pattern of traits, ideas, and behaviors is always present and gives definition to the rhythm. I have found six themes common to organizations that learn fast:

- Make proficiency an organizational priority.
- Be impatient with wasted activity.
- View employees as consumers of learning.
- Stress simplicity.
- Innovate to learn.
- Cultivate candor.

The rhythm always begins with the first theme, a core belief that proficient workers represent a significant business advantage. The remaining five themes are played out differently, highlighting many unique approaches toward creating a breakaway.

Make Proficiency an Organizational Priority

Integral Solutions Corporation (ISC) is a high-energy software start-up in Silicon Valley. Like many other companies in this part of the country, ISC has visions of greatness as it frantically attempts to create a software product that will immediately capture the interest of consumers. So much can be learned from the inner workings of companies like this because of their extraordinary focus on creating and delivering a high-quality product or service to customers, especially from the strategic importance these companies place on proficiency.

Colin Earl, the British-born software savant who founded ISC, is very deliberate in his actions to find and develop people. In a conversation we had in his San Jose office, he outlined a start-up's version of high-speed learning. "One thing in our company that is absolutely clear is the consequential relationship between revenue and payroll," he said. "When I hire someone— whether a software engineer or an administrative assistant—the person must be able to deliver what we have promised to the customer, or our entire operation is put in jeopardy. Nothing, and I mean nothing, is more important to me than our employees' ability to perform effectively. In our company, every one of us initially has two responsibilities: first, we must personally invest and find a way to come up to speed fast, and second, we must become one of the sources for others to learn from. We are producing software twenty-four hours a day with our global team of U.S. and Russian programmers. If we can't bring people up to speed fast, we die. It's about that simple."

When I asked him to describe his method for rapidly developing workers, he jumped up, walked to a dry-erase whiteboard strewn with scribbling of random notes, and wiped a spot clean. *We clearly know what we are trying to accomplish,* he wrote, and then said, "Everybody knows what we are in business for and what roles they play in making this happen. Our business strategy can be experienced through the excitement of each new sale and often seen in the tired eyes of our programmers. What we have promised the marketplace is very important to us, to our future and to our egos. If we can't deliver, our first priority is to find a way and learn how to do it."

In a second freshly erased spot on the board, he wrote, *We know what part of our delivery process is most vulnerable.* "Today, our software developers must be able to program in Java, Perl, and C++. Without this, our commitments will be missed. We also know that our salespeople must be able to articulate our value proposition in the context of a customer's network architecture. Fluency in these two areas is our learning priority because it places us at the competitive crossroad between success and failure."

In another tight spot on the far right side of the whiteboard, he wrote, *We ask people how they want to learn.* "Absolutely nothing impedes us from giving people the flexibility to learn in the method they choose," he nearly shouted. "The only caveat is that they choose a method that drives them to performance fast. This usually takes the form of a rapid introduction and acceleration into practice sessions."

Finally, he wrote, *We measure and reinforce learning speed.* "We pride ourselves on the fact that we can have a new employee contributing value in a very short period of time," he concluded. "In fact, this is the essence of entrepreneurial organizations. Some of this has to do with our size, but most has to do with our attitude toward learning and performing."

This kind of focus is typical among companies that have separated themselves from the competition by making proficiency an organizational priority. Learning in these companies is given the same importance as other key strategic investments. Training efforts in organizations that dance to this beat are in lockstep with immediate business needs and are not managed as isolated activities or events to schedule during downtime. Most, if not all, of these organizations use business metrics to measure their progress. The Balanced Scorecard, discussed in Chapter Three, is becoming an increasingly popular tool to integrate learning with an organization's strategic goals, along with measures such as financial performance, customer satisfaction efforts, and internal cost management.[4]

Be Impatient with Wasted Activity

People in these organizations want to break away from the pack, and nothing frustrates them more than a slow, bureaucratic system for training. Their central belief is that they can learn faster, and that belief promotes actions that make faster learning possible. Workers talk of knowledge and learning in the context of customers, market share, and profit. "New knowledge and improved performance" is their mantra, and they thrive on learning, anytime and anywhere. They aren't afraid of trial-and-error learning; in fact, they relish it—the faster, the better. In this environment, facilitators and instructors are focused on performance and results. Their ultimate goal is developing skilled and proficient employees, not planning training events or scheduling activities.

A mid-sized customer relationship management software firm in Silicon Valley, strapped with the challenge of selling and implementing a new version of its software delivered five months late, illustrates how impatience with wasted activity can spur employee development. The truth is that the managers of the firm were forced to try something drastic to develop their sales and support staff: not only were they nearly half a year behind with the rich new software features, but their typical development process for technical sales representatives would have added another four months to the process. At that pace, they would have missed the crucial fall sales cycle that makes or breaks enterprise software companies.

Two feisty leaders were tagged with preparing the technical sales team for the fall sales season. They had two weeks. One of the leaders was from the software engineering team, and the other was a technical sales lead; both lacked experience in instructional design or training. On a dry-erase whiteboard that ran the length of one wall in the cafeteria, they crafted a strategy using cartoons. Beginning on the left side of the expansive wall was a headlike icon with a big question mark on its forehead. Below the icon was the question "What do you already know about version 3.*x*?" The tale then moved through a sequence of colorful hand-drawn icons and statements depicting this story: "Identify what you already know so we don't waste time, pick the top five features, attributes, and value propositions" (they had a list of sixteen), "and match those with the software developers that built them; the software developers will become your coaches. After you find your coach, jump on the computer and immediately begin trying to use the software and demonstrate its functionality." Awards were given for the biggest blunders and screw-ups in an attempt to entice fast failure. Stock options were awarded to one wide-eyed sales manager who inadvertently locked up the entire company's test server.

Witnesses to this process described it as absolute disorder and chaos. The tone of the description, however, was not critical but complimentary. Nearly one hundred sales-related professionals, in three physical locations, lived through this procedure. Within two working weeks—in this company, twelve days—the sales team was fully prepared to sell and support the new release of software. The key ingredient in this free-for-all process of training was fun-filled reinforcement for rapid cycles of failure: the faster learners fail, the faster they can learn. Impatience with wasted activity clears away the dead wood of the traditional training process and allows learners to reach proficiency fast.

View Employees as Consumers of Learning

Jinny Goldstein, former president and CEO of PBS The Business Channel, has a vision and a passion for what she dubs "the learner-centered environment." She also has the character and the presence to command the attention of the toughest audiences. When she describes the future in terms of creating an environment specifically to meet the needs of different learners, people listen. Goldstein envisions a virtual "learning-neural system" that surrounds a worker with options for content, delivery choice, and reinforcement that erases the line between work and learning.[5]

> People in these organizations want to break away from the pack, and nothing frustrates them more than a slow, bureaucratic system for training. Their central belief is that they can learn faster, and that belief promotes actions that make faster learning possible.

Isn't it odd that Goldstein is considered visionary? If employees are not the decision makers on how they wish to learn, then who is? The learning-neutral system that Goldstein and other visionaries refer to is less complex than it sounds. The for-profit PBS subsidiary The Business Channel, which recently merged with the National Technological University (NTU), must sell its content to a wide array of different learners. If learners are considered consumers of how they want to learn, then providers need to develop a whole range of delivery options: not only do we all learn in different ways, but we each need to learn in many different situations. Today, NTU and The Business Channel provide learners the choice to consume new information and training online, by CD-ROM, video, collaboration with an expert, and a satellite downlink to a traditional classroom. The key in this interconnected system of delivery is that learners choose the delivery best suited for their current situation and the way they believe they learn best.

Organizations that have achieved the rhythm of speed to proficiency view employees as the consumers of all learning investments. This idea reflects a crucial shift in perspective that opens enormous opportunities for faster learning. Today's employees browse the Web, absorb the news, and converse with customers, internalizing a vivid picture of the changes taking place around them. Even when away from work, they continue to consume information—learning has become second nature to them. This strategy recognizes that when the learning methods in the workplace are out of sync with those in the world outside the corporate walls, learning becomes contrived and unnatural and ultimately slows to a crawl. Fast-learning organizations take advantage of the abundance of information and technology available outside the workplace; they reap the reward of faster learning by synchronizing with the daily, natural learning of their workforce.

Decision makers in fast-learning organizations also understand that workers must want to learn before there is any chance of application. Therefore, they attempt to identify the individual learning needs and preferences of workers and to fashion learning activities that can quickly translate into knowledge applied on the job.

Stress Simplicity

Making the connection between simplicity and speed is a common attribute among companies striving to reach proficiency faster. Organizations that are making the learning process simpler in order to speed up knowledge acquisition do not break a complex system into its component parts.[6] Instead, they start with a simple system and resist the urge to create a rigid, engineered system for learning.

The field of instructional design has its roots in the scientific method and engineering principles. When I was working as an engineer in the aerospace industry, we had a saying, "If in doubt, build it stout." This concept is prevalent in our conventional training processes as well. We typically design training to handle the biggest load for the broadest array of learners while packing in the most information possible. Stout training systems take forever to build, and they are heavy, lethargic processes once complete. These courses are counted in days and take enormous infrastructure to employ. In contrast, breakaway training design needs to start with the notion that short, nimble courses should be more like the blades of a disposable razor: once they are out of date, they are tossed away and the next short course is snapped on. The information that is embedded in these small vignettes is housed more than likely in the corporate intranet or a content management system that keeps it current. Speed therefore comes from the rapid extraction of this information through unorthodox and simple methods, including search engines with remediation and quizzes integrated with the information, satellite synchronous brown-bags lunch sessions with a specialist or an instructor, and on-the-job practice to ensure that threshold proficiency is reached. These creative methods are more focused on the knowledge needs of today, knowing that tomorrow will bring information we have yet to anticipate.

Simple also comes in smaller pieces and modules. Organizations in today's competitive economy can't afford to put their employees through lengthy training sessions or wait for them to complete a full course before they are able to bring new skills and knowledge to their jobs. Shorter learning modules allow workers to achieve a specific learning objective quickly and to begin using new knowledge immediately. "The smallest teachable unit" is the goal for Patrick Hernandez, vice president of New Century Energies, a large utility provider in the Rocky Mountain region. "We can design, develop, and teach a one-hour module in the time it takes to design a one-day course." Hernandez helped lead the merger between Public Service of Colorado and a large utility provider in northern Texas. "The only way to bring two management cultures together was to keep the learning process as simple and flexible as possible."[7]

Flexibility is a sibling of simplicity. A fixed method for delivery and reinforcement begs for complexity in design and implementation. Flexibility requires forethought and a bias toward the less complicated. As one teacher put it, "The new facilitator guide must help me stand in front of a class, talk to a video recorder, shrink the key contents into a reinforcing voice-mail message, and announce the availability of all three on our Web page." Finally, the companies that get full return from their simple approach have a bias toward authenticity and try to dispel the ambiguity that arises from overly complex instructional design and methods. The more rigid, inflexible, and contrived the materials, the more difficult they are to explain, the greater the possibility for inconsistencies to emerge, and the more likely that the reasons for learning will be obscured.

Innovate to Learn

My young son and his friend recently found a way to use SEGA and Nintendo video game controllers interchangeably. The process wasn't pretty, but it allowed them to get more players in the video game without buying additional controllers. Although I am certain that the manufacturers would be concerned about this, I am also certain that the manufacturers don't view technology like my son does. He and his friends have coined a new word, *technovate*, to describe their experiments, which use technology as a commodity and their minds as the ever-increasing source of innovative ideas.

Payoff from advances in technology will come when we use it in ways never before imagined. When used intelligently, today's information technology (sometimes called IT) can dramatically reduce the cycle time to proficiency, rapidly advancing an organization. Specifically, improvements in desktop multimedia and Internet-intranet applications promise innovative applications in learning. This powerful new class of information technology offers extraordinary strategic advantage to those who use it creatively. As precise as a surgeon's scalpel, today's technology enables an organization to pair an individual with the right content at the right time. For the first time in history, we have virtually eliminated the barriers of time and space for linking workers with new information.

Unfortunately, many companies are using this new capacity merely to automate methods already used in conventional training. Making information continuously available to workers through innovations in technology takes courage from leaders. As nervous as access to the Internet makes many decision makers, it is Internet browsing that transforms a worker from someone who waits for formal training into a proactive, curious learner. Now that information is available in various forms of multimedia, the responsibility for learning and ultimately performing can be placed where it belongs—with the worker.

This advantage alone should persuade cautious decision makers of the advantages of adopting a serious information technology delivery strategy. An enterprise today is defined by its use of information. *Connectivity,* the new buzzword, is the key to leveraging today's technology. Information and the mechanisms for delivering it link people together. Access to this information will facilitate a person's ability to learn and act quickly. From interactive kiosks arranged to accommodate the manufacturing flow of a factory to handheld devices for airplane mechanics working in tight spaces, the technology that allows us to quickly find or receive information is now ubiquitous. In an environment where the opportunity for development comes in transient spurts, technology affords workers the means to reach proficiency despite the physical constraints of the operation. The ability to log into a learning session whenever time is available and in a readily accessible environment is a boon to all the workers whose situation previously made it difficult to participate in training. Perhaps the most powerful lever of "anytime, anyplace" learning is the fact that it allows a business to tie the learning process directly to the value proposition. If the initial learning is juxtaposed with the accumulation of experience in the workplace, workers can instantly integrate a short technology-based session with their performance and immediately practice using the newly acquired knowledge and information.

Cultivate Candor

"If we can't ask the tough questions and take on the obstacles that are keeping our people from learning fast, then how can we expect our business to improve and grow?" asks Sam Reese, vice president and business development guru of Kinko's.[8] He believes that honesty about training that isn't working is the ultimate catalyst toward learning faster.

Leaders in companies that are seeking speed to proficiency put the training process and budget under the same microscope as all other important growth efforts. In these companies, employee training and development is no longer viewed as a separate institution or some sacred method that cannot be questioned. Instead, employee development is looked at in terms of capacity planning, market introduction, and overall performance cycle time, receiving the same scrutiny as any other key part of the operation. Truthfulness regarding the process that develops the people of an organization is not a negative activity. Like any other critical part of a company, continual evaluation and improvement of this process are vital parts of any management system.

Rarely are all the obstacles removed before we move ahead, but the people in fast-learning companies courageously ask tough questions about why things aren't working, and the obstacles to learning are the first to be scrutinized. Workers challenge the assumptions about learning that slow them down, and they would rather expose these false assumptions than ignore them. Being unafraid to see things as they really are allows organizations to explore new and better ways to reach proficiency. They may err toward the practical, but their businesses can more quickly and thoroughly implement new

> Organizations that have achieved the rhythm of speed to proficiency view employees as the consumers of all learning investments.

technology and distance-based instruction than companies chasing the latest fad. Few of these companies have a training department that is separate from the core business. If they have a leader of learning—a chief learning officer, for example—he or she sits at the same table as other officers in charge of the corporate growth initiatives. Tom Kelly, Cisco Systems' vice president for worldwide training, is not only responsible for transforming the way Cisco manages its internal training programs but also sweats the operational details of an operation that generates many millions of dollars for Cisco. Kelly is part of a new breed of learning leaders that are assuming key roles in fast-moving corporations.

He represents the business of having people learn and perform faster, and like any other successful leader, he views the training process through realistic and candid eyes and constantly works to make it something better.

The Breakaway

In all of the fast-learning companies I examined, these six themes combine in such a way that each company seems to dance to a different beat. However, all the companies that champion the message of this book have found a passionate, high-speed *rhythm* for reaching proficiency faster. Ultimately, creating a rhythm for speed to proficiency produces significant operational advantages. An organization must build the capacity to serve customers more quickly and effectively than the competition. The rhythm, once created, stimulates a number of competitive advantages that are extraordinarily difficult for the competition to duplicate, and that creates the breakaway.

CHAPTER SEVEN

The Leadership Agenda

Taking People from Where They Are
to Where They Need to Be—Fast

> This new agenda will move the center of gravity
>
> of an organization toward the
>
> rapid development of its people.

I received an e-mail message from Steve Berrard, the former CEO of Blockbuster Video, seeking some information from me. Typical of many executives with little time and much to do, he ended the message with the words, "Send me the executive summary." This chapter is for people like Steve Berrard in leadership positions with much to do and not enough time to do it all. Like any fundamental change, creating a breakaway requires sustained, inspired leadership. In this closing chapter, I want to speak directly to you as a company leader and discuss how your agenda needs to change if your organization is to profit from the breakaway. Here is an executive summary of the leadership agenda:

• Leaders are the only people in an organization who can establish a new vision for the way their employees learn. We're not talking about learning for learning's sake but rather something that is at the heart of the firm's mission and its ability to prosper: the power to deliver value to customers—fast. It's up to you to make sure that everyone understands and believes this.

• Articulating this goal is only the start: if you take the idea of breakaway seriously, you must literally rethink what you're doing as a leader. The breakaway agenda must drive your daily activity and become a leadership mantra.

• The corollary is this: responsibility can't be delegated. Making speed to proficiency a priority doesn't mean giving the job to someone else, even a high-level person. It means walking the walk yourself and making sure your co-leaders do as you do.

• You must no longer think of training and development as a cost to be managed, a drain on the company resources. It's an investment as necessary as providing workers with equipment they need to do their jobs—with a much greater rate of return.

The leadership agenda is changing once again. The focus of the past five years was on restructuring costs, preparing for Y2K, and developing strategies for growth. Today, growth is still the overarching agenda topic, but one of the biggest problems facing leaders with aggressive growth targets is how to develop their organization's social fabric so that it can learn at breakneck speed. My recent discussions with business leaders indicate that "the organization" has moved back onto center stage. Leaders, specifically CEOs, are beginning to take more seriously some of the training and development concepts that they recently supported only nominally.

This shift is partly a logical next step for companies that have completed the necessary cost restructuring and infrastructure development for e-commerce. Leaders must now look to revenue growth for the next leap in performance, and this growth can come only from customers. To a large extent, the renewed emphasis on the organization coincides with a movement to reintroduce the employees of the enterprise to its customers. The fizzle of the dot-com notion that eyeballs can replace revenue as the primary driver of value only reinforces the agenda of preparing the organization's people to propel growth. Leaders seeking to capture differentiated growth in revenue through the proficiency of their "organization" are establishing a new agenda. This new agenda has four principal themes:

- Creating an obsession for preparing the workforce to compete and deliver value
- Embracing and leading the Net generation
- Attracting and retaining the free agent worker
- Bringing innovation to the development of people

Creating the Obsession

The headquarters of the ServiceMaster Corporation in Downers Grove, Illinois, would surprise most people. Instead of a towering glass-and-brass facility with an imposing lobby—what you might expect for a $5 billion corporation—it is a renovated single-level building with an open foyer. Along with an expansive granite wall on which ServiceMaster's core values are etched, the lobby is dominated by a convex wall of white-framed windows enclosing the company's showpiece: a classroom. This classroom is more than a functional space where many hours of learning have occurred; it is a physical metaphor for what the leaders and people of ServiceMaster believe: their business is developing people.

Every few weeks, you will find chairman Bill Pollard teaching in that classroom. On another day, you will find him learning— from faculty of the Harvard Business School, for example, or from customers who are invited to talk about their products and service requirements or from his own employees and franchise owners.

The fundamental reason for the enormous growth and success of ServiceMaster is its unparalleled drive to develop people. Today this company, possibly better known for its market-leading consumer businesses such as TruGreen, ChemLawn, Terminix, Merry Maids, and American Home Shield, is the world's leading service company, achieving twenty-six consecutive years of growth in revenues and profits. It employs more than two hundred thousand workers and serves more than six million customers in thirty-one countries.

Because of Pollard's obsession, ServiceMaster continually builds value by developing smart, professional workers and placing them in front of customers. The company's success is not based on taking up some recent training fad or using a new technology but on an unwavering commitment to make employee development its top priority. Pollard listens, learns, and teaches every day. His actions set the leadership expectations at Service-Master. At the beginning of a teaching session, for example, he asks his audience: "Am I prepared to serve as I lead, to listen as I promote, to learn as I teach, to commit as I expect others to follow, to build on the ordinary as I expect the extraordinary, and to develop people as I seek to grow profits?"

What most distinguishes leaders who can continuously spark organizations to succeed and prosper from those who cannot is their fierce commitment to learn, to teach, and to develop people. A corporate leader's thirst for listening, learning, and applying new knowledge produces a cascading effect throughout the organization. Through their own actions and behaviors, such leaders create a dynamic culture of knowledge sharing and teaching.

One sales employee of Buckman Laboratories, a leading chemical company located in Memphis, described his company's obsession for learning: "Discovering new information and sharing it with everybody is as popular and career-advancing here as a good golf game was at my previous employer. Bob [Buckman] defines our culture. His leadership in the area of learning and knowledge management influences all of us, and because of his tenacity in building 'The Knowledge Network,' we are believers and practitioners."[1] Long a leading light in the knowledge management movement, Bob Buckman now has a system at Buckman Laboratories that brings associates in over eighty countries together to share knowledge in solving customer problems. Leaders like Buckman forge a new way of doing business and establish the benchmark through their own learning activity.

Bob Galvin of Motorola is another leader with a passion for learning and teaching. He made Motorola a global leader in the production of high-quality electronic products at a time when Japan was eating nearly every other American manufacturer for lunch. Today, in his senior years, he continues to be obsessed with helping Motorola employees learn and compete. I was working at Qwest when I had the opportunity to hear Galvin, in his role as Motorola's chairman, explain the methods Motorola used to reach a world-class position. At the time, Qwest was in the process of establishing a leadership council to address business issues concerning learning and training, and our chairman, Richard McCormick, invited Galvin to speak to the leadership team. The obsession and passion we observed in the venerable, confident Galvin changed the way many of us viewed our priorities and our people.

He began his address by discussing the way Motorola views its learners, their training, and the cost of developing people. "Training at Motorola has never cost us any money because the cost of *not* training far outweighs any cost associated with it. If we train a person on SPC [statistical process control] in the first quarter and it costs $500, we know that person will be at least $500 more productive in the second [quarter]. We also know that our current cost [because] of poor quality is far greater than any cost associated with training. This thinking is axiomatic for us, and some may say I am presumptuous about the results. If you don't believe that your investment will pay off in this way, it won't. I have a few doubters. I tell them to look at my numbers—and I don't hear from them again."[2]

Galvin's unabashed belief in employee development and learning inspired all of us who listened to this sage business leader. Because of his intense desire to create a workforce that could compete with that of any engineering or manufacturing company around the globe, his team responded accordingly, and the company achieved world-class status.

An obsession for developing proficiency means also making it a top priority. Phil Condit, the accomplished leader of the Boeing Company, found time to complete his doctorate in engineering while tackling the largest aerospace merger in history. Through his personal example, he demonstrated to his organization the belief that knowledge and proficiency will take Boeing into the third millennium as the leader not only in commercial aerospace but in engineering, manufacturing, and assembly knowledge as well. This has long been his guiding philosophy, and Boeing continues to attract and develop the best engineering and assembly talent on the planet.

These examples illustrate the critical first step for you as a leader of a breakaway. The obsession must begin with the leader. If the passion is authentic, it becomes infectious, and the organization positions itself for the breakaway.

Leading the Net Generation

Expertise requires education, and much of what we have known as education and employee development is changing before our eyes. The way it is funded, designed, managed, and delivered will change more in the next few years than it has in the past century. The first evidence of this change is the dramatic acceleration of technology, especially the growth of the Internet as a tool for learning. Today's technology and the inherent ubiquity of the Internet have cut down the traditional barriers of time, space, and cost. Workshops, seminars, customized training events, and competitive information previously available only to companies with abundant resources are now available to anyone with Internet access. The economics of learning are changing fast, and small, nimble companies can now obtain new information and reach proficiency following an affordable cost model. The emergence of online education and information is not only a matter of technological change but also of access. "Anytime, anywhere" access to information, content, and methodology will enable workers to develop a new orientation to time and space as it relates to their learning and development. Reaching proficiency will become a continuous process that replaces onetime training events.

But technology is not the only movement behind the recent advances in learning. The people who work with that technology, especially young people, are key. For the "Net generation," a group of young adults so comfortable with technology that they think it is all part of the original plan, life and learning without a technology twist is simply unthinkable.[3] Armed with the will to learn and an intimate knowledge of current technology, they will be a formidable force, and a positive one, for organizations that foster a youthful culture. These "kids" are just now entering the job market. Along with their predecessors, the digitally literate Generation X, they will soon represent the majority of workers in the service and technology sectors of our country.

Leading this new generation of workers requires an open mind and a little finesse. Luckily, I did not need to go far to begin my own education regarding the potential of this group of people. Avaltus, the organization I currently lead, is a growing software company with more than 40 percent of our workforce below the age of twenty-six. Like their baby-boomer parents, these young people want to have successful careers, raise families, and live fulfilled lives. The way in which they reach these goals, however, will be very different from the path of their predecessors. For nearly all workers before the Net Generation, television profoundly influenced how we saw the world, driving our knowledge of current events, our voting behavior, and our exposure to new products and services. In essence, we developed our thinking and our actions from a media process that sent us information as we passively sat and soaked it in. The Net Generation is the first that will develop in a dynamic, interactive process. These people are thinking, learning, working, and consuming in fundamentally different ways from any other generation. And as learners, they will learn radically faster than any other generation in the company if the new information and "training" that is served to them is highly interactive, up-to-the-minute, and somehow connected to other Net Generation workers.

People in this age group are strikingly intuitive, and they have little fear of trying something new. I recently witnessed a training session where a company was teaching its workforce how to use a new Internet-based procurement system. The classroom had a computer set up for each student, and the instructor—a baby boomer—was methodically walking the students through the software features. One person, somewhere in the forty-plus club, was literally pointing his mouse at the screen like a channel changer. He needed to take the "basic computer skills" course before proceeding. Most of the other students, of Generation X or older, were finding the course helpful. But the three Net Generation students had passed the concluding quiz within the first ten minutes of the class and had established a chat session to pass the time.

Our challenge and our opportunity as leaders is to look at this new generation not as a group of tough-to-manage, overly sensitive youth but rather as insatiably curious workers who can learn new things at the speed of light. They come to their first job programmed to take advantage of technology instantly, and they love the next new thing, thriving on the latest version of software or the newest office gadget. Find a way to attract and retain this group of individuals, and enjoy these dividends:

- Members of this generation learn interactively, and they expect to be constantly learning on the job. They seek more than job security—they expect to be steadily growing, discovering, and learning something new.
- Because they continuously seek the next new thing, they also seek and expect change. They are motivated by the fact that the status quo is dead. This may be the first collective generation that thrives on change and does not resist it.
- These young adults, accustomed to speed and near-instant feedback, are as impatient as your customers. They understand responsiveness and can help you think like a customer.
- Net Generation workers want to participate in the core mission of the organization they are working for. They're ready and motivated to advance the delivery of value to customers—so invite them in.

Attracting the Free Agent Worker

A few years ago, *Fast Company* magazine, in an issue titled "Free Agent Nation," declared that there was a "movement" across the nation's workforce called "free agency."[4] The issue and the reinforcing articles described a group of workers, some 25 million strong, made up of approximately 14 million self-employed, 8.3 million independent contractors, and 2.3 million who work each day through temporary agencies. For leaders who are attempting to build a highly competitive organization and one that can rapidly change and deliver value to customers fast, pay close attention to free agency.

Whereas most members of the Net Generation enter organizations as their first job, the typical free agent is a seasoned, highly successful professional. Many of these people became free agents because they were not completely fulfilled in their corporate careers, because entrepreneurial juices drove them to go it alone, or because they wanted to have more control over their calendar and living location. Whatever the reason, the free agent contingent is rapidly expanding, and a savvy leader will attract this group to augment the organization. What's important for a leader to recognize in free agents is that they are intrinsically motivated to bring instant value to the organizations they serve. They continuously invest in their specialty and are often past the threshold level of proficiency; value delivery can therefore be nearly instantaneous.

These new workers play a critical role in helping organizations learn and deliver value fast. Recently, I was on a conference call with one of our customers who provides reservations software to the lodging industry. The purpose of the call was to design a method to train a new group of workers how to use one of this customer's standard software applications. The company had in the past trained hundreds of people to operate its reservations platform; this time, however, the customer was a hotel in Chile. The training would need to be translated and delivered in Spanish, and the hotel had to have the new system operable, with fully proficient call center representatives, in 130 days.

Thirty minutes into the call, I realized that of the seven people on the call, three were free agents. For example, the coach responsible for training the customer service representatives was a recent retiree of a successful Chilean retail firm, where she managed a large inbound call center. Her job was to help with the overall design of the training and to prepare a team of coaches for the eventual development of the customer service representative. This was her first assignment as a free agent, and from her enthusiasm it was clear that this would be a successful undertaking. What she brought to the table was fifty-three years of bilingual existence, many years of call center leadership acumen, and a catalytic dose of free agent excitement. Another free agent was responsible for translating the English version of the courseware into a Chilean version of Spanish. She had been independent nearly all of her career but brought enormous value because she had translation experience from a wide array of businesses and projects. The project manager, the person who would track and manage all of the details of the effort, was also a liberated corporate worker. He received his project management certification when he worked for Lockheed Martin and now introduced himself as the CEO of Project Perfection, a sole proprietorship. These three individuals offered more than professional expertise: they were the key ingredients to meeting the short deadline and helping this growing software company acquire and retain a customer in a new market.

The free agent is an important stakeholder for leaders who choose rapid cycles to proficiency. The Net Generation worker who enters your company programmed to learn fast and ready to jump into new technologies does not bring the knowledge and experience of the typical free agent. The two together, however, are something to behold. Where the youthful twenty-year-old will push the incumbent worker with unbridled youthful zeal and spunk, the free agent will pull the bulk of the organization with experience and immediate value. As a result, the people sandwiched between the two will ultimately change, learn, and deliver value faster.

No doubt our constantly changing business environment will require leaders to keep their heads up and pay attention to other "movements" of today's workers. When you combine the free agent movement with the dramatic changes in the demographics of today's workforce, you will see that the fundamental reshaping of the current system for training is inevitable. Independent corporate refugees seeking to put their loyalty and experience into the project instead of the company can be a critical constituent to any organization attempting to create the breakaway.

Bringing Innovation to the Development of People

Innovation has long been the hallmark of market-leading companies. Invention and ingenuity in product development, packaging, marketing, and technology have created significant opportunities and growth for companies that can "out-innovate" their competition. As important as product innovation and improvement have been to the success of a business in the past, however, the most important innovation today is in the development of people. For all the advances we have realized in manufacturing technology, telecommunications, and computing, little has changed about the learning process in corporations.

Injecting innovation and energy into the learning process can awaken the sleepiest of organizations. A purposeful, innovative act from a leader can spark a learning revolution and transform an organization struggling with change. Jerry Johnson is the senior vice president of operations for Safeguard Scientifics, a hugely successful firm that has enabled companies like Novell, Cambridge Technology Partners, and the Internet Capital Group (ICG) to grow successfully, leading ultimately to successful initial public offerings (IPOs). Prior to joining Safeguard Scientifics, Johnson ran one of the largest field forces in the telecommunications industry: more than thirty thousand employees in fourteen states worked in his operation. In 1994, Johnson was responsible for a major reengineering effort that had fallen seriously behind schedule and was faltering. The newly designed processes were not producing sufficiently to meet customer demand, the computer system upgrades were months behind schedule, and the confidence of the workers was declining rapidly. When Johnson asked his senior management team to diagnose the problem, it was clear they were out of touch with the workers, who were desperately trying to meet commitments and serve customers. Most managers were attempting to solve problems from a knowledge base that was obsolete and in many cases actually ran counter to the reengineering effort.

A wacky, innovative learning idea changed all that. Johnson, who had also been a teacher and educator, decided that *the members of his leadership team needed to become students and relearn how to run the business—from the workers who were doing it.*

In a letter to his leadership team, Johnson initiated a process that would ultimately transform his team, the workers, and customer service. Johnson's letter called for the leadership team to undertake what might be called a "mission of discovery" about the company to allow these leaders to "rediscover and learn from the collective knowledge of your employees by joining your fellow leaders in studentship. The method will require courage to admit the unknown, hard work to learn again, and willingness to allow employees to guide your studies and impart their knowledge to you. The result will place you in a position of leadership, not of weakness, and build a relationship with employees, a relationship we need to move this organization forward. It is time for us to get back in touch with the core of this business and lead it forward."[5]

Johnson designated a two-week period for this "study mission" and instructed his executives and managers to clear their calendars. He told these colleagues that they would be traveling by bus to selected operational sites and "listening and learning from our employees." To ensure that the visits to the company sites would "get below the typical cosmetic surface of prepared presentation and discussion," Johnson kept the itinerary of the journey a secret. He explained that the group would be "traveling to places rarely seen and talking to employees who may have strong opinions. Treasure is in the unknown and uncomfortable."

In his letter, Johnson laid out the ground rules for his team:

I require five behaviors from each of you:

- Admit to not knowing—"I recognize there is a lot I don't know"
- Be a buddy—learn to rely on each other
- Use discipline—adhere to agreed-upon guidelines and norms
- Exercise "studentship"—become a student and a teacher
- Be willing to change—act upon new learning

A bias to learn requires genuinely seeking out information, ideas, and feedback that may run counter to our current assumptions. If our current leadership culture is one of always having the information and answers, we will never change fast enough to survive. Courage to listen and admit the unknown is our first step in becoming the leaders needed to run this organization. Instead of being perceived as weak, we will begin to build respect and rapport with our workers.

Learning to depend on others and to be reliable and trustworthy is an integral part of this mission. One cannot survive the trip without the assistance of a "buddy," just as a business cannot survive without an authentic relationship between the management team and the employees. Building this relationship starts with your own team. As in the real world, not all information is given to you. Seeking to know and understand is the behavior that will open our currently closed minds. For example, you may know where the morning meeting place is, and your buddy may know the time. A responsible buddy checks to make certain his or her partner is on the bus when departing, has the study guide for each visit, and meets all conduct guidelines. Additionally, your buddy will become a confidant and counselor for the exhausting days of our discovery. Imagine our management team supporting each other in this way every day. Becoming a veritable buddy starts to break down the facade of "knowledge is power." In this case, knowledge is potent only if combined with your partner's information. This study mission will expose the impact of combining the collective wisdom of employees with the insight of the management team, our system for the future.

Johnson wanted his study group to develop and agree on a strict set of behavioral norms—conduct necessary to sustain congeniality and goodwill while spending nearly sixteen hours a day together—and he proposed fines for anyone who violated those norms. "The amount of money is not the central idea behind the fine but rather the commitment made to each other and personal pride to uphold the commitment." His buddy system was designed to strengthen the reliability of each individual. "Finding someone to rely on and to be reliable to accelerates learning about yourself and your buddy. Without a reliable buddy, adhering to all the behavioral agreements is nearly impossible."

Johnson concluded his letter with these words: "Finally, the commitment to act and change following the study mission must be resolute and made before our first lesson. If you have any doubt that this mission will help us learn and run this organization better, let me know now. After our employees have exposed their hearts and minds to us, we must act upon their teaching and make the necessary changes. If we don't, never again will they believe management to be genuine or trustworthy. The knowledge we will gain during this study mission is powerful enough to transform any company, business, or organization. I trust you all will join me in this important effort."

Johnson's invitation must have been perceived as bizarre. Most of these executives usually traveled on a corporate jet, not a bus. All had climbed the corporate ladder as experts in their respective fields. Hopping on a bus to learn from the rank-and-file was probably not an idea they had encountered before. As skeptical as these executives may have been before the trip, however, they are believers today. For many, not only did the trip transform their leadership approach and overall knowledge, but it also changed their lives. They experienced the richness of leadership as learners and found hundreds of new sources of information to help them make better decisions. And as for speed to proficiency, nothing compares to the real-time experience of this kind of mission.

Although innovation is a core business discipline critical to any organization's success—indeed, it is considered the heart of America's preeminence in entrepreneurship and business—it has yet to be applied in any meaningful way to the development of workers. The learning process in the vast majority of organizations today is a tired relic of the command-and-control era of half a century ago. It did not work all that well even then, and today it likely does organizations more harm than good. Providing a sourcebook for innovation is beyond the scope of this volume; but if an organization begins with the proposition that the primary purpose of developing its people is to deliver value to customers fast and that nothing will be allowed to get in the way of that promise, leaders will pursue innovation in the development of workers with the same vigor that they pursue innovation in products, processes, and delivery, and that innovation will change the face of American business.

Leading the Breakaway

I believe that the new agenda in this book will move the center of gravity of an organization toward the rapid development of its people. Successful leaders will be those who can organize and accelerate this development, not only for the benevolent reasons of lifelong learning and development but also for the hard-line competitiveness of the firm. As the leadership agenda continues to develop, the natural question is whether the focus is the right one. From my perspective, the new agenda is properly directed not because great minds created it but because business survival will demand it. Remember, the individuals who lead their organizations to break away from the competition will enjoy market share and revenue growth never before imaginable. But the key to the breakaway is a proficient workforce that can deliver on its promises to customers—fast.

INTRODUCTION

1. The 287 interviews that form the foundation of this book were conducted between February 1993 and March 2000.

CHAPTER ONE

1. Robert H. Schaffer, *The Breakthrough Strategy: Using Short-Term Successes to Build the High-Performance Organization* (New York: HarperBusiness, 1988), pp. 11–18.

CHAPTER TWO

1. Peter F. Drucker, *Post-Capitalist Society* (New York: HarperCollins, 1989), pp. 32–40.

2. According to *Training* magazine's 2001 Industry Report, American companies with more than one hundred employees spent a total of $56.8 billion on training.

3. G. V. Goddard, Wickliffe C. Abraham, Michael C. Corballis, and Geoffrey K. White (eds.), *Memory Mechanisms: A Tribute to G. V. Goddard* (Mahwah, N.J.: Erlbaum, 1991). Goddard's insights follow the pioneering work of Hermann Ebbinghaus; see his *Memory: A Contribution to Experimental Psychology* (New York: Columbia University Press, 1913), trans. Henry A. Ruger and Clara E. Bussenius. For additional information about learning and memory, see John R. Anderson, *Learning and Memory: An Integrated Approach* (New York: Wiley, 1994).

CHAPTER THREE

1. Robert S. Kaplan and David P. Norton, *The Balanced Scorecard: Translating Strategy into Action* (Boston: Harvard Business School Press, 1996), pp. 73–76.

2. A number of sources document Deming's teaching on the internal customer-supplier relationship. One of the best is Kaoru Ishikawa, *What Is Total Quality Control?* (Upper Saddle River, N.J.: Prentice Hall, 1985), pp. 73–88. The best source for a definition of the value delivery chain can be found in James B. Quinn, *Intelligent Enterprise: A Knowledge- and Service-Based Paradigm for Industry* (New York: Free Press, 1992), pp. 198–205.

CHAPTER FOUR

1. John Dewey, *How We Think* (New York: Prometheus Books, 1991), p. 52. (Originally published in 1910.)

2. Dewey, *How We Think,* p. 53. Italics added.

3. Robert M. Gagné, *Studies of Learning: 50 Years of Research* (Tallahassee: Learning Systems Institute, Florida State University, 1989), pp. 533–537.

4. Anderson, *Learning and Memory,* pp. 190–209.

CHAPTER FIVE

1. Christopher Meyer, *Fast Cycle Time: How to Align Purpose, Strategy, and Structure for Speed* (New York: Free Press, 1993), pp. 17–23.

2. Henry E. Riggs, *Managing High-Technology Companies* (New York: Van Nostrand Reinhold, 1983), pp. 95–97.

3. Richard B. Chase and Nicholas J. Aquilano, *Production and Operations Management: A Life Cycle Approach,* 5th ed. (Homewood, Ill.: Irwin, 1989), pp. 516–521.

4. Quinn, *Intelligent Enterprise,* pp. 349–351.

5. Frederick F. Reichheld, *The Loyalty Effect: The Hidden Force Behind Growth, Profits, and Lasting Value* (Boston: Harvard Business School Press, 1996), pp. 122–125.

6. Howard Schultz, *Pour Your Heart into It* (New York: Hyperion, 1997), p. 125.

7. Interview at Smoky Hill Starbucks, Aurora, Colo., Nov. 11, 1998.

8. Schultz, *Pour Your Heart into It,* p. 128.

9. The estimates given on Starbucks' learning speed come from interviews with Starbucks employees conducted between Nov. 11, 1997, and Feb. 15, 2000. Partners were interviewed during their breaks at Hyde Park in Sydney, Australia; King Street in Toronto, Canada; Clark and Madison in Chicago, Illinois; Central Avenue in Albuquerque, New Mexico; and Smokey Hill in Aurora, Colorado. These partners volunteered their experiences as learners within the Starbucks' operation. Using their information as a baseline, I calculated that creating the menu of coffee-related drinks takes nearly ten minutes in initial attempts but that partners can dramatically reduce that time through successive practice. They estimate a 5 to 10 percent improvement with each practice session. This rapid rate of improvement levels off when one can produce an espresso-based drink in less than two minutes. Fluency, however, requires this

performance while under the pressure of waiting customers. This research was not sponsored or funded by the Starbucks Corporation or by its management. The interviews were on a volunteer basis by willing partners.

CHAPTER SIX

1. Eric Ransdell, "IBM's Grassroots Revival," *Fast Company,* Oct.-Nov. 1997, pp. 183–185.

2. Interview with Janet McAllister, IBM vice president of global learning, Sept. 1997.

3. Interview with Paul Nichols, director of training at Arrow Schwebber, Inc., Aug. 1997.

4. Kaplan and Norton, *The Balanced Scorecard,* pp. 126–143.

5. Interview with Jinny Goldstein, CEO of PBS The Business Channel, Mar. 1999.

6. Margaret J. Wheatley, *Leadership and the New Science: Discovering Order in a Chaotic World* (San Francisco: Berrett-Koehler, 1994), pp. 75–79.

7. Interview with Patrick Hernandez, vice president of human resources, New Century Energies, Feb. 1998.

8. Interview with Sam Reese, vice president of Kinko's, Oct. 1997.

CHAPTER SEVEN

1. Daniel H. Pink, "Free Agent Nation," *Fast Company,* Dec. 1997–Jan. 1998, pp. 132–150.

2. Bob Galvin, chairman of Motorola, speaking at US West, Oct. 1995.

3. Don Tapscot, *Growing Up Digital: The Rise of the Net Generation* (New York: McGraw-Hill, 1998), pp. 3, 75–77.

4. Pink, "Free Agent Nation."

5. Courtesy of Jerry Johnson, June 1995.